FASHION
PRINT DESIGN
from idea to final print

FASHION
PRINT DESIGN
from idea to final print

Angel Fernandez

A&C Black • London

First published in Spain 2009 by
Parramón Ediciones, S.A.
Rosselló i Porcel, 21 9ª planta
08016 Barcelona

This English edition first published in Great Britain 2010 by
A&C Black Publishers
36 Soho Square
London W1D 3QY
www.acblack.com

ISBN 978 1 408 12489 5

EDITORIAL DIRECTION: María Fernanda Canal
EDITOR: Marta R. Hidalgo
ART DIRECTION: Mídori
GRAPHIC DESIGN AND MAKE UP: Pilar Cano
TRANSLATION: Luke Moreland
DIRECTION OF PRODUCTION: Rafael Marfil
PRODUCTION: Manel Sánchez

6 INTRODUCTION

8 DEVELOPMENT OF THE PROJECT the creative process

10 **THE STUDIO OF THE DESIGNER** the tools and materials of work

14 **THE CLIENT**

18 **RESEARCH AND DOCUMENTATION**

26 **THE NOTEBOOK** laboratory of ideas

30 **INSPIRATION** moodboards

34 **INTRODUCTION TO COLOUR THEORY**

38 **THE MOTIFS**

42 **DEFINING THE IDEA**

46 **DEVELOPMENT OF THE COLLECTION**

50 **TRADITIONAL AND DIGITAL TECHNIQUES**

58 FROM THE IDEA TO THE PRODUCT the technical process

60 **PRESENTATION OF THE DESIGN**

64 **POSITIONAL PRINTING AND** *RAPPORT*

72 **TECHNIQUES**

76 APPLICATION OF THE DESIGNS ONTO THE FABRIC the final result

78 **THE RAW MATERIAL**

96 **DYES, VARNISHES AND PIGMENTS**

98 **FINAL PRINTING PROCESSES:** screenprinting, devoré, digital printing, embroidery, roller printing, thermotransference, block printing, resist printing

124 **THE FINAL PRODUCT**

130 STYLES AND MOTIVES gallery

132 **BOTANICAL GARDEN**
Flowers, foliage, romanticism, pop inspiration

140 **GEOMETRY**
Lines and circles

146 **SPORTING LIFE**
The sea, the mountains, the city, the countryside

152 **FAIRY TALES**
The stories of fairies and the fables

158 **NOAH'S ARK**
Real and imaginary animals

166 **EXOTIC TRIPS**
Africa, Asia, South America

172 **LETTERS AND NUMBERS**
Ideas and messages

178 **ART**
From Baroque to the Bauhaus and the Abstract

186 **NEW ROMANTIC**
designs from the imagination

190 INDEX AND ACKNOWLEDGEMENTS

As a product of the art and the creative genius of fashion designers, the collections that every season reach the the public stage are valued according to two basic dimensions: the pattern making and the raw materials or textiles. A good knowledge of these two dimensions will provide the designer with the maximum freedom to represent his or her ideas and will contribute towards consolidating the designer as a creator with a distinct identity. As the famous motto of the teacher Cristóbal Balenciaga goes: 'the fashion designer must be an architect of lines, a sculptor of form, a painter of colour, a musician of harmony, and a philosopher of measurements.' In this context, designers work with a series of techniques and processes to create, to give, to sculpt, to decorate, to draw and to treat the textile.

However, even though it seems obvious that fabrics are part of the basics of clothes, the creation, development and manipulation of the materials are aspects that generally remain hidden in the art of fashion. It is also true that from fashion chains' collections of *casualwear* up to the most exclusive *haut couture* creations of Paris, printing is a basic part of the work of every designer. Because of this, a simple T-shirt can assume a unique identity and can even manage to be converted into a piece of cult fashion thanks to the appearance of the graphic motifs that are applied to it. That's why printing is a process that not only requires skill and creativity to define the motifs, but also knowledge of the techniques and possibilities that exist to apply them onto the raw material.

DEVELOPMENT OF THE PROJECT
the creative process

THE STUDIO OF THE DESIGNER
the tools and materials of work

The influence of the atmosphere around the designer is a key factor in the creative process. Because of that, the designer's work space should not only cater to the need for organisation and movement, but also reflect his world. This studio should be, therefore, a surprising area full of magic that invites inspiration.

A well-structured work space must always have good ventilation, some good views, and a space for relaxation. As for the furniture, it is important that it be equipped with desks of sufficient size, ergonomic chairs, and a library for organising books, magazines, catalogues and movies.

Powerful digital equipment is another basic component. The computer will need to have a large scanner and a printer, and it is also useful to have an integrated photocopying machine.

Generally, textile designers combine classic and digital techniques, which allows for a greater range of effects.

The great quantity of materials that one uses requires shelves to store for example, watercolours, inks, pencils, paintbrushes, gouache, sprays, etc., as well as an area for cleaning tools and equipment. Every company or studio has a different layout.

There are companies that have their own textile design department and others that use external designer studios. The studio can be complete with a workshop where one can make silk screens and test the fabrics, although this space is not an obligatory condition, since this part of the creative process can be carried out in external workshops especially set up for such purposes.

Normally, a studio of designers consists of several people directed by a creative director who assigns them projects and is in charge of the follow-up. In the same way, every design studio has a different form of organisation, and it is possible to find teams in which everyone works individually on different projects.

1. The organisation of the tools is fundamental for the development of the job.

2-3. The studio of textile designers Lise Gulassa (California) and Cyrille Gulassa (Austria). From the firm Sisters Gulassa.

WORK TOOLS AND MATERIALS

A deep knowledge of artistic materials and their creative possibilities is important in enabling the designer to employ a wide range of techniques to represent ideas. If the designer gets used to only using a single technique, he or she will probably find it difficult to satisfy the demands of different customers. That's why it is important that he or she has good equipment and materials and a knowledge of how to use them.

GRAPHITE PENCILS
These are the basic tools most often used to produce drawings. The pencil is formed by a mixture of pulverised natural graphite and clay that has been baked to a specific temperature. According to the hardness of the lead a bigger or smaller proportion of graphite-clay is used. The more clay, the greater the hardness.

The hard lead pencils contain a dry lead of greyish tone that is a little narrower. The softest have an oily lead, fragile, dark and thicker. The graphite pencil is the best means to draw monochrome figures with linear lines that underline its profile.

MECHANICAL PENCILS
Mechanical pencils have a push button that allows the release of the lead, or graphite, to control the length one uses. Their application is varied in the different phases of the design. They can be used with a lead of 0.5 mm for sketching or to scribble ideas in a notebook, or with leads of 0.3 to 0.9 mm that, besides being useful for the first states of the drawing, allow a greater quality and precision in the details. They also offer the advantage of not having to be sharpened. As with conventional pencils, the leads come in a variety of hardnesses.

PASTELS AND THE CHARCOAL PENCIL
Pastels are composed of dry pigment pulverised and mixed with a combining agent. The resulting paste forms the bars or leads of the characteristic colour. This tool is nearest to pure colour, because there are almost no foreign elements in the pigment. The charcoal pencil is constituted of powder mixed together with a greasier agent that allows a thick and intense stroke.

COLOUR PENCILS
Pencils with colour leads provide subtle lines as well as vivid strokes. They are very clean and they hardly need maintenance. Their handling does not differ too much from the conventional pencil. Only two aspects should be taken into account: the stroke can not blur and its greasy consistency prevents complete erasure with a rubber. According to their material of manufacture, the colour pencils are presented in several categories, including watercolour.

FELT-TIP PENS AND MARKERS
Felt-tip pens constitute the most modern technique of drawing and are especially useful for illustration or publicity projects. The process of work with felt-tip pens is similar to that of colour pencils and they offer splendid results when they are both combined. The felt-tip pen has a structure similar to the pen, since it contains its own ink. The tip of the felt-tip pen is usually made of a porous material, such as felt.

INKS AND PAINTBRUSHES
Ink is a liquid substance with a high depigmentation power capable of providing a clear stain, with contrast and precision if it is thick, and a sinuous, transparent and delicate quality if its intensity is reduced with water. Chinese ink – one of the oldest varieties – is the thickest. The pigmented inks, for their part, contain other components, such as varnishes, to ensure the adherence of the pigment to the surface and to prevent its erasure by mechanical abrasion. These materials are generally resins (in solvent inks) or composites (in water inks).

COLOUR INKS AND WATERCOLOURS
The technique of watercolour is based on the effects of transparency that allow the pigment to be diluted in water when settling on the white surface of the paper. This same principle is the one that guides work with colour inks, also known, among the designers, as aniline or liquid watercolours. In general, they are applied with round paint brushes.

GOUACHE AND ACRYLIC
Gouache and acrylic paints share many characteristics, even if their constitution is very different. They are both soluble in water, although once the acrylic paint dries it is permanent and presents a glossy brightness. Gouache, on the other hand, allows better cover once dry. It is matt and can only be dissolved by passing a wet paintbrush over it. Both paints work with paintbrushes, round as well as flat. In spite of the resemblance, both paints should never be mixed on the same job.

DRAWING MATERIALS: PAPER AND NOTEBOOKS
Paper is one of the most recurrent tools used by fashsion designers, although in the presentation of the projects this can be accompanied by samples of fabric and supporting textures that complement the design. The choice among the wide variety of papers available depends on the medium that will be used for the drawing. The grease-proof paper – fine, translucent, very soft and with a waxy surface – is the most useful. Because it is a paper with transparency, it is often used for transferring templates and images.

CAD EQUIPMENT *(computer-aided design)*

Computer-aided design (CAD) permits the introduction of images (original or scanned photographs) and allows them to be manipulated later with drawing and finishing touch programs. The possibilities are almost infinite. These methods are faster and cleaner than the previous ones, but their application requires knowledge of the available design computer programs. The uses of these tools vary from applications based on vectors and systems of drawing in two dimensions (2D), up to pattern makers in three dimensions (3D). They consist of a geometrical database (points, lines, arcs, etc.) with which one can operate to interact through a graphic and variable interface.

1. Pencil drawing done manually and coloured with inks. From the firm Ailanto.

2. Composition carried out on a computer with images taken from books. It is printed on a grease-proof paper (tracing paper) in order to draw with graphite pencil.

3-4. Sketchbook featuring watercolour flowers, and a box with Chinese paintbrushes of different thicknesses.

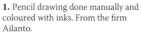

1. The creations of Divinas Palabras
were aimed at a young public, informal
and intellectual, who pay attention to
the printed message on the garment.

THE CLIENT

When designers have their own textile firm, they do not have restrictions – except the market – regarding to whom they want to direct their business or to the type of designs that they can carry out. However, this is a comparatively rare situation. Generally, it is the client who will determine the direction that the designs will have to take, from the moment in which the client decided on its public objective and a style. In these cases, it is the fashion or fabrics firm that commands the work of the designer. If the assignment comes from a fashion firm, the designer will have the profile of their customer beforehand. Thus, the project will depend then on the final purchaser of the garment: their age, sex, social status, purchasing power and style (sporting, classic, luxury, etc.). The targetted public is usually, therefore, a segment of the population selected according to these characteristics and with a level of homogeneity. Much of the success of the design will depend on the extensive knowledge of this segment of the population.

The goal of the designer is to satisfy the wishes of the clients. But of course, always from his or her own personal vision and style, which is, all in all, the reason why the client has chosen this person to carry out the design of the clothes line in the first place.

2-3-4. The work of the textile designer Marcus James adapts to the requirements of the different commercial firms. These designs and the final applications on the garment are assignments for the brands Yves Saint Laurent (collection 2008) and Camilla Staerk (Fall-Winter 2006 collections and Spring-Summer 2007).

Faithful to her style, the textile designer Hanna Werning has developed a concept line that has been applied to garments and accessories for the firm House of Dagmar in the different seasons.

The applications of ribbons, fabrics and embroideries have been chosen as the connecting threads of the designs that compose the first Alta Costura collection in Paris of the designer Josep Font.

RESEARCH AND DOCUMENTATION

Few creative activities require being always aware of the latest trends as much as that of the fashion designer. Either to follow the direction of the trends or to mark a totally divergent personal style, the designer must constantly be alert, acting like a coolhunter, always compiling all the information of the present.

In their search for inspiration, the designers must investigate constantly. They must keep their eyes open to the various channels of information in the world of fashion (Internet, parades, fairs, books, museums, stores, market trends, etc.), assimilate the subtle aesthetic changes and observe the behaviours and tastes of the people.

So, as far as the trends are concerned, the designer must scrutinise the immediate environment on-the-fly in search of subjects or motifs to incorporate into their designs. However, it is also of extreme importance to be aware of the new fabrics and techniques of printing. In this sense, the Internet offers an almost infinite world of information. A good way of obtaining a great selection of images of interest is to get in touch with websites which specialise in fashion and trends, such as www.wgsn.com, www.instyle.com, www.stylesight.com, www.fashiontrendsetter.com or www.trendunion.com, among others.

On the other hand, magazines, other publications which specialise in fashion, and the trade show catalogues help design and styling professionals keep abreast of the movements of the big fashion house designers in the main fashion centres of the world (Paris, London, New York, Milan). If the designer has the opportunity to travel, he or she can attend design events such as parades, fairs and trade shows dealing with fabrics and accessories. It is a way of keeping in touch, all in all, to the varied sources of the fashion industry.

Websites which specialise in fashion are a necessary tool if the designer wants to be up to date with the last trends.

The personal library of the designer is an inexhaustible source of inspiration.

THE TRENDS

A trend is a pattern of behaviour of the elements of a particular environment during a specific period of time. In less abstract terms, it refers to the things that are in fashion, or that are about to be in fashion. Being aware or ahead of trends relies on the intuition of the designer, joined with the information that the environment offers. These themes will mark the guidelines about what the designer should work with.

The creative textile designer always works one step ahead of the fashion of the street. From the moment in which he or she elaborates the designs, a season will go by before the product arrives on the trade circuit. That's why it is vital that the designer knows in advance what the so-called 'fashion of the street' demands. Sometimes the designer is capable of predicting the trends but the market is not ready yet for them. In those cases it is better to keep the ideas for the future, although there is always the possibility of presenting them in the more avant-garde sectors.

The specialised trade shows, which take place in the main centres of fashion production, are other sources of valuable information for the designer. This type of event allows one to see the trends at least a year ahead, to establish contact with the sources of the fashion industry, to compile first-hand the relevant innovations to the charts and forecast of colours, the types of fibres and fabrics, and the new lines for the creation of garments for man, woman, child, etc.

Another way of keeping up to date is to access the reports from the numerous fashion professionals who travel around the world compiling data to publish in fashion magazines, or reports for firms in the sector. In this field there are departments which specialise in predicting the trends for the different areas of fashion and textiles. These professionals offer designers ideas on the colour, the textures, the motifs, the silhouettes and other aspects that will be trendy in the coming seasons. Some designers prefer to remain on the margin of the trends and of all this information, and work according to their personal tastes and intuition without letting the market influence them, perhaps thinking of a more exclusive public or with the intention of being the precursor of a new style or trend.

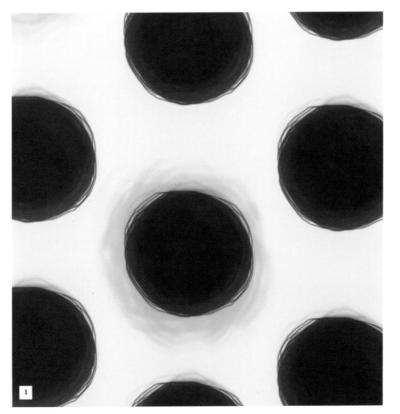

1. The polka dots are a motif that the trends take up through the different seasons in versions according to each period (WGSN).
2. The digital treatment of the figures gives rise to multiple visual effects that the designer uses to generate variants on the same drawing (WSGN).

3. The traditional motif of the swan acquires a new dimension thanks to the use of the digital techniques. From Marcus James for the firm Camilla Staerk.
4. The designs that are shown on the catwalk are influential in the brands of the high street to create trends that arrive for the general consumer. From Marcus James for the firm Camilla Staerk.

1

2

1. Exhibitions of international interest can be influential in fashion, as it has happened on repeated occasions with the Japanese artist Utamaro, whose drawings are printed on this handkerchief of silk.
2. Figures inspired by Japanese culture have always been found in trends because of the appeal of their delicate forms and the combination of colours.

3. Detail of Japanese kimono in silk painted by hand.

4. Illustration carried out with the technique of templates and spray, often used on street art. From the firm Ailanto.

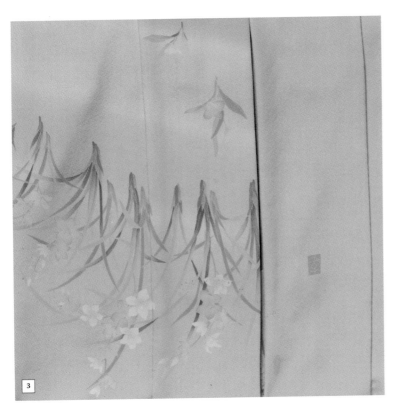

3

4

Details of prints on silk for wedding kimonos. The floral motifs and the geometry are recurrent inspirations for Japanese creators.

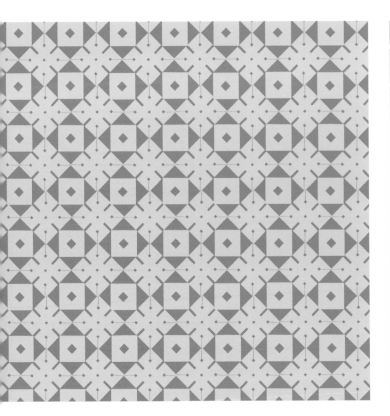

THE FAIRS

Twice a year, before the following seasons: Spring-Summer and Fall-Winter, textile shows present the latest trends and innovations in woven and printed materials. These exhibitions are, at the same time, a platform for designers and an area in which creative people can show their work and sell it to textile manufacturers and designers. One of the most important fairs in this area is celebrated in Paris and is called Première Vision (www.premierevision.fr). Textile manufacturers and designers from around the world are brought together in the French capital to buy and sell their products or to see at first-hand the novelties of the sector.

Parallel to this exhibition, other meetings take place such as Expofil, dedicated to fibres and spinning; Le Cuir à Paris, dedicated to skin and leather, and Indigo, which specialises in textile design, printing, embroideries, and vintage materials. As important as that in Paris is the fair which is celebrated in Florence, Pitti Filati, subsidiary of the exhibitions of Pitti Immagine, which is also attended by experts from around the world (www.pittimmagine.com).

Other important textile shows celebrated every year in different cities of the world are:

PREMIÈRE VISION NEW YORK: preview of trends in fabrics. New York (United States). www.premierevision-newyork.com

PREMIÈRE VISION MOSCOU: preview of trends in fabrics. (Moscow, Russia). www.premierevision.ru

TEXWORLD: latest trends in fabrics. (Paris, France; New York, the United States; Mumbai, India). www.textworld.messefrankfurt.com

SALÓN TEXTIL INTERNACIONAL DE BARCELONA: presentation of the principal collections of fabrics. (Barcelona, Spain). www.stib.net

IDEABIELLA: fabrics for fashion for men and women. (Milan, Italy). www.ideabiella.it

IDEACOMO: fabrics for feminine fashion. (Milan, Italy). www.ideacomo.com

MODA IN: vanguard materials for the market of fashion. (Milan, Italy). www.fieramodain.it

PRATO EXPO: innovative fabrics for the casual fashion for men and women. (Milan, Italy). www.pratoexpo.com

SHIRT AVENUE: fabrics for shirt making. (Milan, Italy). www.shirt-avenue.com

MUNICH FABRIC START: international fair of fabrics. (Munich, Alemania). www.munichfabricstart.com

TECHTEXTIL: international monographic fair. (Atlanta and Las Vegas, the United States; Frankfurt, Germany; Shanghai, China; Mumbai, India; Moscow, Russia).

INTERTEXTILE: fabrics for dress making and furniture. (Beijing and Shanghai, China). www.messefrankfurt.com.hk

YARN ESPO: international fair of fibres and yarns. (Shanghai, China). www.messefrankfurt.com.hk

PITTI FILATI: knitted fabrics. (Florence, Italy). www.pittimmagine.com

A similar motif, such as the arabesques, is presented through a large number of variants thanks to the application of different techniques of drawing and printing. These designs from the firm Lissa were shown in the fair Première Vision Paris, Winter 2008.

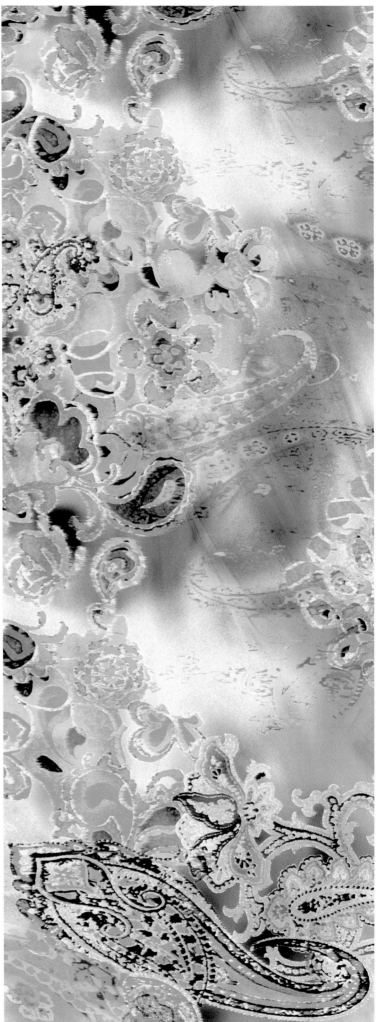

THE NOTEBOOK laboratory of ideas

The notebooks or sketchbooks are the first step in the process of creating a print. In them ideas are represented, creating something similar to a visual journal in which some concepts are highlighted that will be accepted or discarded with time. The sketchbooks are a space for testing and where the ideas materialise in drawings. They are a personal file in which the images that come to the designer from numerous sources: museums, magazines, parades, movies, books or the street itself are stored.

The sketchbook includes the necessary conceptual material to complete an idea about printing. This includes: design, colour and three-dimensional pieces. Any object is useful if it provides something new and interesting – from a newspaper clipping to a sample of fabric, the leaf of a tree, and even photographs of characters, trips or the environment. This sketchbook contains pieces of great visual appeal by themselves and with an eloquence that converts them into the best tool available to the designer to view the creations before making them public.

It has to be taken into account that at first the drawings,

notes and designs developed in a notebook are not for public consumption. Because of that, they constitute a a place where the designer can work without inhibitions or outside judgments, and thus they are suitable for creating the boldest designs.

A sketchbook contains very personal information of the designer. This information can generate new and original ideas and, because of that, it must not be revealed in a premature way.

There are several ways of sketching ideas, but the most common is by using a pencil, for the drawing is an important part of the process of design. In these drawings, the stroke must be agile, doodled, synthetic and not very precise.

Generally, it is not conceived as a perfect illustration, but as a sketch that only the author himself can endow with meaning.

1

2

3

4

THE DRAWING

Drawings in the *sketchbooks* lack elaboration because their principal mission consists of reflecting an idea. The goal of these sketches is to sketch a line, to comprise in an abbreviated form indications of style or colour.

It is for this reason that most of these drawings are executed with great speed, which in turn gives greater spontaneity and freshness to the stroke. The drawings, although sketched, must be easily legible or interpretable for the author, for their goal is to clarify ideas and concepts.

For many designers, the sketchbook must have complete digital support, not only because their ideas and information come from the computer – either through the Internet or from images that they collect with the digital camera – but also because they can develop the drawings using computer programs.

Although it is true that the computer makes available a large library to be inspired by, as well as infinite possibilities for effects that would make the pencil, paper and cutouts unnecessary, the excitement coming from its novelty has passed. At present the trend is to go back to the classic techniques as far as drawing is concerned.

To remember and to process better what has been observed, the designer refers to notes written on the margin of every drawing. This way one can add information about the colours, textures and tonal values. These annotations are necessary for preliminary presentations to the customer or to the tailor. Thus, in these cases, the sketches are accompanied by appendixes with sentences that show important details, subjective impressions such as dates, localities, indications of colour, points for the embroidery, or types of fabric.

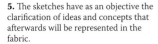

1-2-3-4. The *sketchbook* is a visual journal in which the first concepts of a print are reflected accompanied by notes with specifications on textures and colours.

5. The sketches have as an objective the clarification of ideas and concepts that afterwards will be represented in the fabric.

Research on variations of motifs of the same colour in drawings carried out with aniline and bleach, from the notebook of Javier Nanclares.

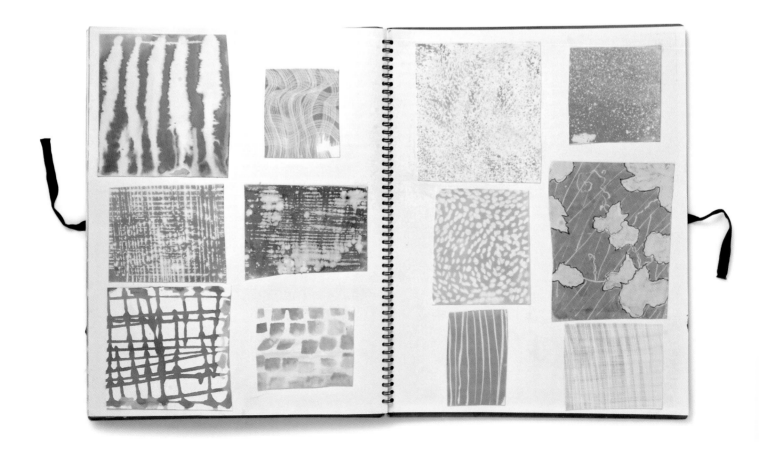

The same motif drawn by hand on paper (**1**), a digital drawing (**2**), and the prototype on a garment (**3**).

INSPIRATION moodboards

Inspiration is combined with constant research that obliges the designer to keep his or her eyes open to the channels of information in the fashion world in order to assimilate the subtle aesthetic changes they reflect. We could say that a designer is like radar that perceives the variations of the period and the concerns of the immediate environment and incorporates them into the designs.

The process of compiling materials and images is a key step in the creation of motifs. For that, the designer uses a moodboard that accompanies and complements the sketchbook and that brings together suggestive images on the chosen subject. This panel of trends acts as a source of inspiration as well as a tool to generate and to connect ideas.

The moodboard is a composition, carried out in paper or in digital format, which includes the visual lines that have inspired the creation of a motif for its future printing. It is a collection of images extracted from magazines, books, the Internet and photographs that, as a whole, give an idea about the style one wants to attain. This board of information which contains photographs of gadgets, garments, cutouts of fabrics, colour charts and daily objects that have been cut out and put carefully in order, enables the grouping together of different ideas in one double page. Once sufficient images have been compiled it is possible to start to develop new designs. With time, these moodboards, based on collages, can turn into a useful reference file to which the designer can go to in order to extract or recover ideas.

COLOURING

In order to define colouring, the most universal language is that of the Pantone (the company responsible for creating physical colour charts for the professionals). The Pantone colours that are used in the world of the fashion are those of the finish TC (Pantone Textile Colours). When the designer delivers the original drawing to the workshop, the company producing the fabric will be in charge of finding the most accurate colours based on the Pantone colour reference number or real samples of the colour.

Moodboard for inspiration created on a photobase. Original collage of Javier Nanclares.

As if they were a *patchwork* of ideas, moodboards reveal the designer's sources.
Collage of fabrics of wild silk accompanied with photographs of *Vogue Italia* as referents of style.

Moodboard for World Global Style
Network (WGSN) colouring.

Colour chart
for the Winter season of 2008-2009
of a commercial firm.

Colour charts on the fabric constitute a
more exact approach since the textures
can cause tonal variations.

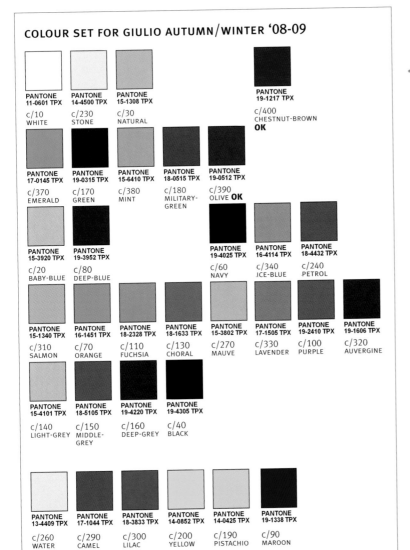

COLOUR SET FOR GIULIO AUTUMN/WINTER '08-09

PANTONE 11-0601 TPX	PANTONE 14-4500 TPX	PANTONE 15-1308 TPX		PANTONE 19-1217 TPX
c/10 WHITE	c/230 STONE	c/30 NATURAL		c/400 CHESTNUT-BROWN **OK**
PANTONE 17-0145 TPX	PANTONE 19-0315 TPX	PANTONE 15-6410 TPX	PANTONE 18-0515 TPX	PANTONE 19-0512 TPX
c/370 EMERALD	c/170 GREEN	c/380 MINT	c/180 MILITARY-GREEN	c/390 OLIVE **OK**

PANTONE 15-3920 TPX	PANTONE 19-3952 TPX		PANTONE 19-4025 TPX	PANTONE 16-4114 TPX	PANTONE 18-4432 TPX
c/20 BABY-BLUE	c/80 DEEP-BLUE		c/60 NAVY	c/340 ICE-BLUE	c/240 PETROL

PANTONE 15-1340 TPX	PANTONE 16-1451 TPX	PANTONE 18-2328 TPX	PANTONE 18-1633 TPX	PANTONE 15-3802 TPX	PANTONE 17-1505 TPX	PANTONE 19-2410 TPX	PANTONE 19-1606 TPX
c/310 SALMON	c/70 ORANGE	c/110 FUCHSIA	c/130 CHORAL	c/270 MAUVE	c/330 LAVENDER	c/100 PURPLE	c/320 AUVERGINE

PANTONE 15-4101 TPX	PANTONE 18-5105 TPX	PANTONE 19-4220 TPX	PANTONE 19-4305 TPX
c/140 LIGHT-GREY	c/150 MIDDLE-GREY	c/160 DEEP-GREY	c/40 BLACK

PANTONE 13-4409 TPX	PANTONE 17-1044 TPX	PANTONE 18-3833 TPX	PANTONE 14-0852 TPX	PANTONE 14-0425 TPX	PANTONE 19-1338 TPX
c/260 WATER	c/290 CAMEL	c/300 LILAC	c/200 YELLOW	c/190 PISTACHIO	c/90 MAROON

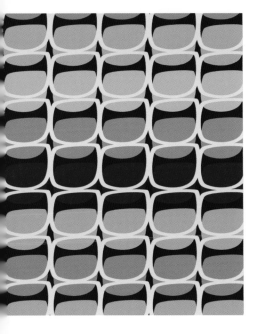

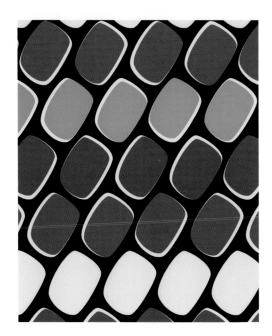

Prints where variations of colour and drawing are shown for the same theme: the optical motifs from a retro inspiration. From Laura Fernández for the firm Simorra. Winter Collection 2008-2009.

JAVIER SIMORRA
Barcelona
PRINT DETAILS
SPRING- SUMMER 09

RAPORT SIZE

35 CM

30 CM

Technical data with colour references

	BACKGROUND	COL/ 1	COL/ 2	COL/ 3	COL/ 4	COL/ 5
OPT. 1	COL.214	COL.211	COL.212	COL.215	COL.213	COL.215
OPT. 2	COL.215	COL.202	COL.207	COL.205	COL.213	COL.210
OPT. 3	COL.215	COL.203	COL.206	COL.205	COL.236	COL.210

Polka dots of different sizes. From Laura Fernández for the firm Simorra. Winter Collection 2008-2009.

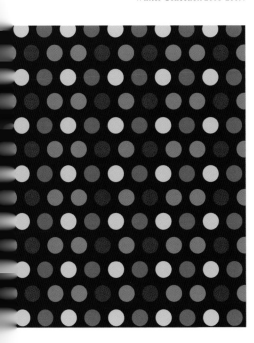
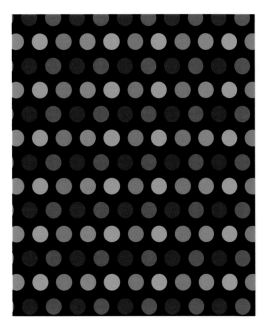

INTRODUCTION TO COLOUR THEORY

Colours are ordered in a graphic representation called a colour wheel, which follows the guidelines of the breakdown of the visible light of the solar spectrum. This classification comes from the interaction of three primary colours (magenta, yellow and blue cyan) that cannot be obtained by combining other colours. This means that they are totally autonomous and they do not resemble any other tone. The mixture of the primaries creates another three new colours (red, green and violet) that are known as secondaries.

The colour wheel is a very useful tool with which to clearly view how the colours interact among themselves and with their complementaries (those that occupy the opposed side of the circle). So for example: yellow is the complementary colour of violet and, therefore, both will stand out more when one applies them together in a design.

When designs are made with a computer, it is necessary to make sure that the colours seen on the monitor are exactly the same ones that will appear afterwards in the design when applied to the garment. For that there are different methods, but the best way is undoubtedly to use specific hardware for that purpose.

RANGES OF COLOUR

Mixing different proportions of the primary colours and secondaries creates new tones. Grouped together by chromatic resemblance they form what is known as ranges. The range of warm colours is composed of those that result from the mixture of yellow, red, ochre and their derived tones: brown, orange, etc. The cold ranges are the result of the mixture of blues, violets and greens. They can become lighter with white dyes and become darker with greys and blues. The range of achromatic colours is formed by the mixture of warm and cold colours. It has greyish tones and is presented as a range with very sober colours. The range of pastel colours, in turn, includes the tones in which the white predominates.

HARMONY AND CONTRAST

The use of both contrast and harmony are basic features that should be considered when designing prints and choosing colours. The effect of contrasting colours prevents boredom and breaks up any possible dullness in the collection. On the other hand, harmonious combinations imply similarity more than difference, thanks to the choice of colours that are not out of place. The most effective way of assuring a harmonious combination is to base it in the analogous chromatic scheme, that is, to follow the order of the adjacent colours on the colour wheel. The use of analogous colours can cover three or four adjacent shades with different degrees of luminosity.

Besides, it is very effective to create forms with contrasting colours that are warm and cold, light and dark, complementary, saturated and achromatic. In this sense, it is useful to take into account that when designing a subtle and slightly contrasted print, the contrast among the colours should be exaggerated slightly, to prevent losing the small nuances.

Colour wheel composed of twelve colours arranged according to the segmentation of the light.

1-2-3. The colours and drawings have a principal role in the configuration of each of these garments belonging to different seasons. From the firm Ailanto.

4. Final drawing with flowers of naïf inspiration and preparation of colours to be printed on white or on any other colour base. From the firm La Casita de Wendy.

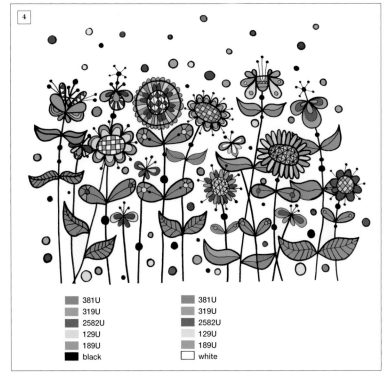

381U	381U
319U	319U
2582U	2582U
129U	129U
189U	189U
black	white

3

1. This vintage illustration painted by hand on silk is used as a guide for the creation of the colour chart that will dominate in a collection.

2-3. Pop inspiration in floral motifs. It presents variations of colour on fabric and drawing by hand of the main motifs on transparent paper. From Laura Fernández for the firm Giulio.

4-5. Prints of camouflage with different tonal variations. The warm colours are combined from the harmony, and the cold colours from contrast. From Laura Fernández for Giulio.

THE MOTIFS

A motif is the graphic interpretation of a concept applied in an isolated part of the fabric or in an organised composition. When the motif has been conceived for repetition, it can be duplicated until it occupies all the fabric. The motifs can be as varied as the imagination of the designer. Anything that has form can be drawn in very different styles, from abstraction up to precise detail.

Floral motifs are one of the most frequent resources in printing for fashion, equal only to geometrical motifs and ornaments. The combination of the forms with the variations of colour creates results of an infinite variety. These results rise up from the imagination of the creator and are realised with the use of the printing techniques.

THE EFFECTS

Textile drawings can modify the perception of the figure, dissimulate the anatomical reliefs and provide a dynamic perception of the piece. Thus, for example, the skirts or dresses printed with horizontal, diagonal or vertical stripes modify the perception of the silhouette of the body, making a person seem wider, thinner, taller or shorter. On the other hand, the application of a motif in specific areas distracts attention from the rest of the garment. This is a factor that the designer will have to take into account at the time of featuring or disguising certain aspects of the figure.

1. White and black drawing for a positional print on a T-shirt. From Laura Fernández.

2-3. White and black motifs with vintage effects for a collection of garments for young men.

4-5. Designs with optical effect composed of the outline of concentric circles and of waved lines.

2

3

4

5

1

2

1-2. The same underlying lines acquire a different emphasis according to the drawing that is applied over them. For instance, in the composition formed by an illustration and a photograph the lines appear more tenuous than in the print with the orchid. By Rafa Mollar.

3. Floral design in soft colours for application on fabric (WGSN).

DEFINING THE IDEA

Before a collection is realised, the designers will have worked a lot on giving form to the artistic concept that underpins and gives value to their creation. The designers will have put their knowledge, intuition, sensitivity and information collected from multiple sources, into practice until they arrive at the idea they want to transmit.

Ideas are even of greater importance today, since competing for price is not an option anymore, and quality and design are the most important features of the collections. The fashion companies have to create a brand and a style that differentiates them, and this is obtained thanks to the ideas of the designer. That's why, before starting to design a collection, it is necessary to develop a line from a source of inspiration. The line should have a design, a range of colours and textures that give it coherence and relate it to a story or concept.

It is convenient to start the process by writing down all the ideas that come up, taking into account the possibilities of creation, originality and versatility that each theme allows for, especially the profile of the final customer: the public to whom the garment is destined. Drawings are a good starting point for arriving at the essence of the concept. Further along, once the sketches start to reinforce an image, one can proceed to add the colours and fabric samples that will complete the representation.

1-2. Each of the prints has been made from an original idea: an abstraction based on decorations from animals and a figurative drawing with scenes of celebrations of high society. From the firm Basso & Brooke.

3-4-5-6. The famous prints of flowers and animals by Hanna Werning transferred to backpacks for the firm Eastpak, collection 2005.

Name: GRASSHOPPER LUCK

Eastpak
January 2004

Hanna Werning
Spring Street Studio

Stockholm / London
+46 (0)70 236 57 25
www.byhanna.com
hello@byhanna.com

3

4

FISHPOND FLUSH

Eastpak
14 February 2005

Hanna Werning
Spring Street Studio

Stockholm / London
+46 (0)70 236 57 25
www.byhanna.com
hello@byhanna.com

5

Name: OCEAN STAR

Eastpak
3 January 2004

Hanna Werning
Spring Street Studio

Stockholm / London
+46 (0)70 236 57 25
www.byhanna.com
hello@byhanna.com

6

Sometimes the work of the textile designer is so transcendant that the customer looks only for the designer's personal style. The well-known cartoonist Hanna Werning has developed prints for the House of Dagmar and Anna Sui, among other firms of feminine fashion.

DEVELOPMENT OF THE COLLECTION

Once the type of business or client for whom the designer will work is specified, the style defined, and the process of research completed, then the designer has a story to describe. The final idea will be translated into a collection in which the designer should give expression to the source of inspiration, the theme of the project and its intentions. The necessary ingredients to develop a collection are creativity, boldness, critical attitude, curiosity, capacity for synthesis, flexibility, innovative spirit, artistic sensitivity and, of course, technical knowledge and knowledge of materials.

It is necessary to display a wide range of ideas that work not only individually, but also show coherence with the collection. A systematic approach to such important factors as style, colour, use of similar prints, and production contributes towards giving this coherence.

The collection requires keeping two visions in mind: one global that makes evident a link with the collection and another with the individual. At the same time that the pieces of the whole collection tell a story, each individual print should contain a unique world that talks by itself. In a collection, 'families' or subdivisions of the central theme, are usually formed which provide a repertoire with different strands within the same theme. The variations can keep the motif as the unifying link and provide different groupings based on the colours.

Also one can employ the same style of drawing with changes in a group defined by the tonality used. Every time that this is done, it is very important to delimit the options so that the idea is reinforced and is not lost in the infinite variables of the design.

1. The colours and lines in the drawings of the dress reflect the global concept of the collection by the designer Miriam Ocáriz.

2. Dress and jacket by Miriam Ocáriz, Summer 2007 collection.

3. Print of Ocáriz used in the Spring-Summer 2007 collection. Once again, the colour and the handwritten lines are made visible; signs that characterise the collections of this creator.

tul plumeti
CAN-CAN +
+
VESTIDO ESTAMPADO

1

1-2-3. View of the evolution of a screenprinted design (see page 103) from the sketch, the garment, and finally, the catwalk. The coherence is the key. From the firm Miriam Ocáriz.

TRADITIONAL AND DIGITAL TECHNIQUES

Only on rare occasions will we find a designer who defines himself or herself with only one working technique. The more tools they master, the more chance they have of obtaining a result that approaches their original idea. The success in the communication of the concept that resides in every collection will depend on understanding the advantages and limitations that the different working methods have. The techniques can be classified into traditional and digital. The first are those that entail a working craft form: inks, watercolours, gouaches and acrylic that involve using paintbrushes or sponges. This category also includes what are called 'dry techniques', such as pencils and pastels, and the oil-based paints (oil paints and oil pastels).

In the traditional techniques one also finds the technique of collage, which allows innovative results through the use of cutouts of photographs, paintings and textures. Finally, another frequently used technique in printing is the *stencil*, which consists in applying the colour with spray or sponge on templates.

Digital techniques are based on the use of the computer, which processes the images and allows their manipulation through specific computer programs. With this tool, the representations can have a done by hand origin or be totally digital. If we choose the first option, the drawing is carried out through the traditional techniques and is scanned afterwards to convert it into a digital file that can be

transformed with programs that enable finishing touch ups of images, such as Photoshop®. This last step provides variations in colours and sizes. With these programs it is also possible to carry out digital collages through the introduction of images derived from different sources. The second option groups together the drawings that are carried out directly on the computer with special programs for these ends, such as Adobe® Illustrator®.

Today, almost all the designers combine the traditional techniques and the digital techniques. The preliminary point of their work is usually a scanned image or photographs that they manipulate digitally until obtaining the desired final result.

Different compositions from the mixture of traditional techniques.

1. Sample that combines the mixture of traditional techniques: gouache, stencil and collage. From the firm Sisters Gulassa.

2. Collage obtained from the cutout of different superimposed fabrics. From the firm Sisters Gulassa.

3. Illustrations done in watercolour. From the firm Sisters Gulassa.

4. Motifs of floral inspiration done using gouache. From the firm Sisters Gulassa

Different compositions from the mixture of digital and traditional techniques.

1. Floral composition with the use of different tones treated digitally. Design of Sisters Gulassa.

2. Different samples of screenprinting on paper from the firm Sisters Gulassa.

3. Different examples in which the combination of traditional techniques and digital techniques results in very attractive effects.

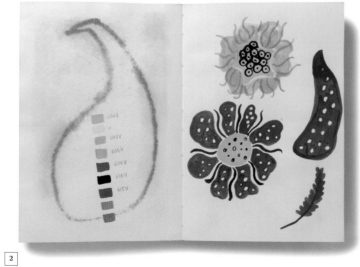

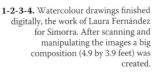

1-2-3-4. Watercolour drawings finished digitally, the work of Laura Fernández for Simorra. After scanning and manipulating the images a big composition (4.9 by 3.9 feet) was created.

5-6. Drawing of floral border with a bird. After completing the sketch the outline was drawn by hand with graphite pencil and, afterwards on a transparent paper, the chromatic characteristics were defined with colour pencils. Both drawings were scanned to create a document with two layers, one for the line and another for the colour. The same motif was sent to India and was embroidered by hand in manila-style on silk satin.

6

THE COLLAGE

In order to make the most of the representation of the designers' creations, they must explore all the techniques that are available, and the collage presents a good resource to stimulate their creativity. This practice consists of assembling different elements in one unified whole. In their elaboration, it makes possible the combination of every type of technique and style. This includes cutouts of images, threads and fabrics stuck on a paper, or combinations of photographs and drawings in a digital document.

This technique is extremely useful in beginning to define the concept. In fact, it works as a means of brainstorming with materials that allows viewing beforehand the combinations of textures, colours, and motifs. Their representative possibilities also convert it into a very good resource to present to the customer with proposals.

1-2. Miscellaneous techniques and materials in collages by Miriam Ocáriz.

3-4-5-6. Drawing and prototypes of embroideries with collage of fabrics, applications, and varied stitches. By María José Lleonar for Simorra.

7-8. Photographic collage, with kaleidoscope effect, from the firm La Casita de Wendy.

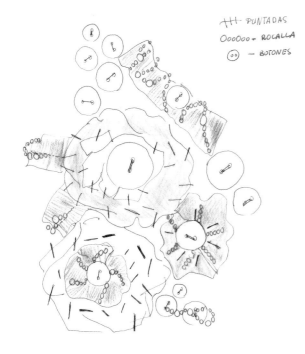

3

4

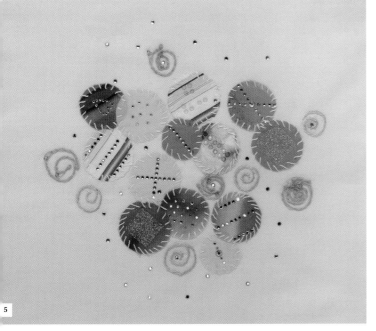

5

6

7

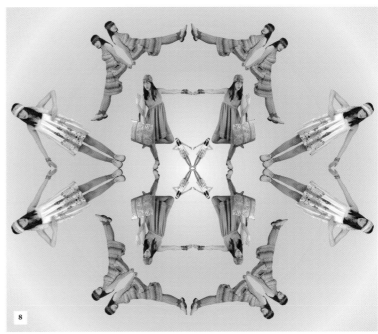

8

FROM THE IDEA TO THE PRODUCT
the technical process

PRESENTATION OF THE DESIGN

The presentation of creative work to the producing company requires that the designer uses an intelligible language to describe all the parts that make possible the translation from ideas into the finished product. The first step of the supplier before starting production consists of providing samples or prototypes of a garment or footage of reduced fabric, following the guidelines marked by the designer. The samples from the supplier will then undergo a series of adjustments for finishing touches, such as colour and intensity, until arriving at the final result. In this way, the designer sets up the mechanisms that prepare the design to be taken to industrial production, separating the colour into layers, creating the crosshatching when it is necessary and the *rapport* if one wants to repeat a drawing in a print. On other occasions, the designer himself is the one who prepares a digital document and a technical sheet in which all the necessary technical aspects for the production are detailed.

In this context, the designer must know the techniques of the products' destination, that is, the different processes of printing that the industry offers. Likewise, it is also very important that one stays updated on the array of possibilities for handling the fabrics that support the designs, such as the dyes and the materials that are used in different processes, since all these factors produce effects very different to the touch and to sight. Besides personal creation, designers can go to special arenas such as the international textile fairs or professional design centres to look for fabrics for their fashion collections. There they can buy original designs carried out by hand, painted on fabric or paper, embroidered, dyed or carried out digitally, all already prepared for delivery to production. Other times only the idea is sold and the designer is in charge of doing the necessary technical preparations for the subsequent industrial process.

Finally, an alternative option consists of purchasing the fabric already finished by a company that is in charge of the creative and technical process, and that presents the product ready to be made into garments.

PANTONE BLACK   PANTONE 5815 C   PANTONE 5005 C   PANTONE 1815 C

1. Detail of the printed motif and its location on the final garment in the presentation to the customer. By Laura Fernández.

2. General view of the garment with the final print.

3-4-5. Technical drawings separated by layers of colour for screenprinting. The separation of colour layers prepares the design technically so that it can be taken to industrial production.

6. Drawing of layers of colour for embroidery.

PRINT 2 brown

3

PRINT 1 BLACK

4

PRINT 3 pink

5

EMBROIDERY

6

SUMMER SEASON 2007 REF:XT-9 POSITIONAL DIAGRAM FOR EMBROIDERED DESIGN

SAMPLE
EMBROIDERED PRINT

11 CM

13.19 CM

BRONZE

4.5 CM

3.5 CM

SUMMER SEASON 2007 REF:XT-11 PRINT AND APPLIQUE

14.5 CM

18 CM

5.8 CM

5.8 CM

FABRIC PATCH

1. The technical sheets include references to the position of the print and the form of application. By Laura Fernández for Xbaby. Collection Spring-Summer 2007.

2-3-4-5. The designer Ligia Unanue creates unique prototypes of garments made of pieces sewn, painted and decorated manually, which she uses to introduce lines to different commercial firms which specialise in clothing for babies.

POSITIONAL PRINTING AND *RAPPORT*

The application of the illustrations is carried out in two ways: situating the image in a sector specific to the garment on a background of full colour, or making the image take up the whole of the piece through the repetition of the original design.

The first modality is known as positional printing and is carried out on the already cut or ready-made garment. This procedure requires that the designer specifies the exact position of the print in the technical sheet with precise coordinates. This type of print can be applied through screenprinting, *hot stamping* or *transfer* and embroideries. Screenprinting requires the preparation of the different layers of colours that will be printed on the *shablón* or mould, whereas the *transfer* cuts back the drawing on a vinyl that afterwards is applied on the garment through heat.

Today these types of designs are very common in the world of fashion and there are many firms that create drawings to decorate their garments. In the past, this type of printing was only common for badges or logos on some garments and in music or souvenir T-shirts. The continuous prints, or *rapport*, are carried out generally through a system of rotary printing, in which a cylinder with the engraving of the fabric spins around the garment and keeps providing the different layers of colours.

Another way of creating continuous prints is by using flat screens in which the top of the drawings are fitted with the lower part to create continuity. If one wants to use this technique, it is necessary to take into account the width of the fabric and of the illustration so that it fits perfectly on the fabric. To achieve this aim, some computer programs, which allow a wide range of manipulation of designs, have been especially designed for this purpose.

1. Technical sheet for T-shirt with positional print. Design of Ximena Topolansky for the firm Strongh Enough.

2. Technical sheet for T-shirt with *rapport*. Design of Ximena Topolansky for the firm Strongh Enough.

3-4-5. Vectorial drawing following a photo scanned of a vintage print. The resulting lines have been filled in with colour to define the main motif. The *rapport* rises up from repeating the same motif in all the directions. From the firm Giulio.

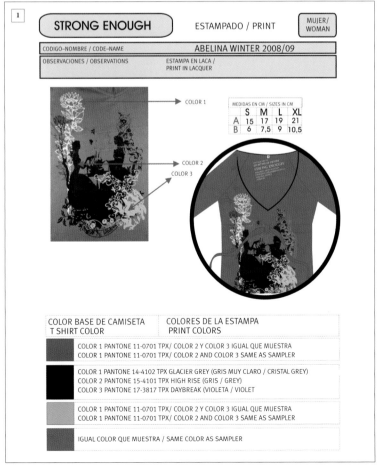

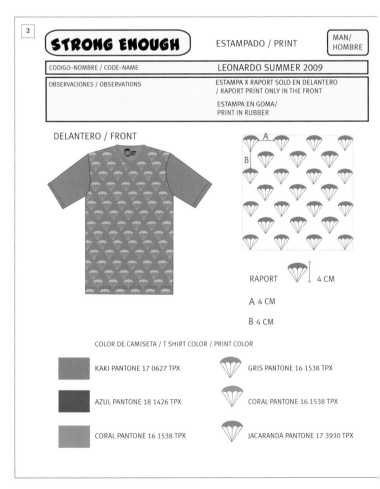

1. Notebook of ideas of Javier Nanclares with collage created with photocopies, photo of the main motif and dry flowers.

2. Drawing with felt-tip pen and motif drawn with black line.

3. Drawing with colour pencils that reflect the interior of the flower carried out separately to create a texture of weaving.

4. Once the drawings 2 and 3 are scanned, a composition is carried out digitally to obtain a continuous print.

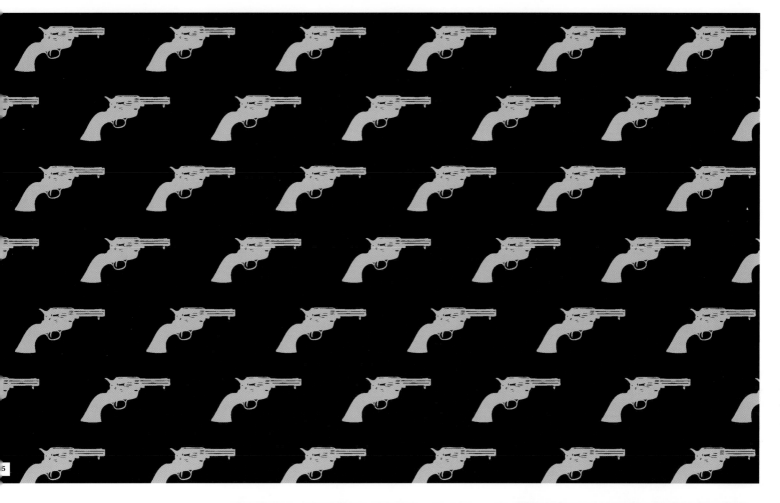

5. Continuous print for men's underwear by Laura Fernández for the firm Giulio.

6. Drawing with heraldic inspiration for a positional print on men's underwear. From the firm Giulio.

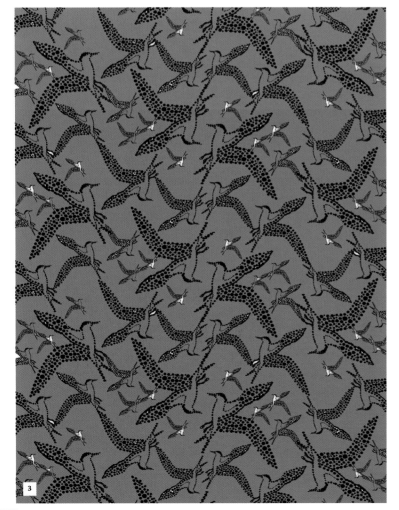

1-2-3. From the same inspiration (the animals), these designs by Paola Ivana Suhonen are applied to the garments as continuous prints.

4-5-6-7. The same theme of Bambi has been developed in different prints. The one that has the underlying rhombuses is a *rapport*, and that of the border around the motif is positional.
By Paola Ivana Suhonen. Collection Spring-Summer 2008.

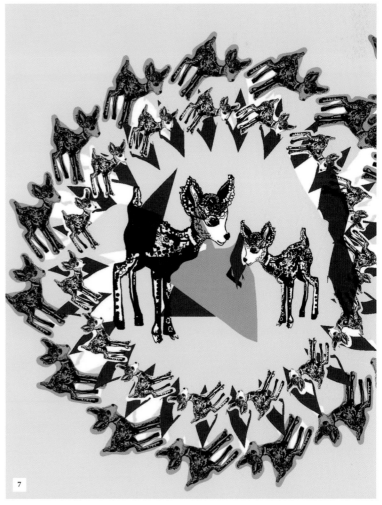

THE *RAPPORT* TECHNIQUE

Rapport is the basic module of repetition of a motif or design for the creation of patterned printing. In other words, it is the basic unit of the design that extends in all directions of the fabric. This composition is carried out from a specific design that is reformulated to obtain optimum repetition.

To create a continuous design there are different methods, but the most used is the one that is carried out through the computer. For that, the motif is first placed in the centre of the document of the work. Afterwards a copy is placed to the right and another to the left of the central motif, forming a diagonal line.

The next step consists in copying that diagonal above and under the central line. This way, a graphic module is generated (with the motif copied nine times) that will lay the foundations for the repetition in all directions.

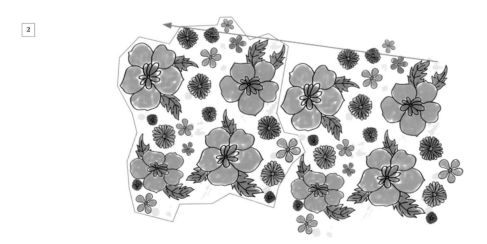

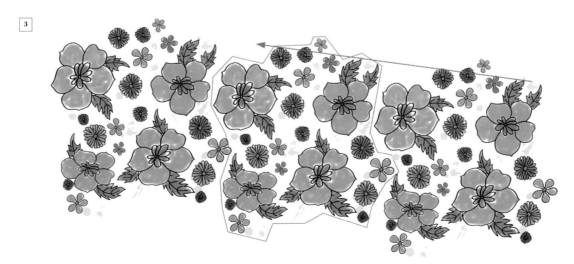

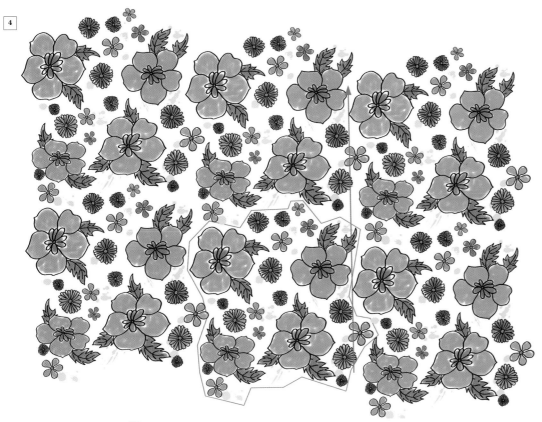

1. Base motif drawn by hand.

2. The scanned base motif is repeated in a diagonal line towards the right to give rhythm to the composition.

3. The same operation is carried out towards the left following the diagonal towards the opposite side, until it forms an inclined line with three motifs.

4. The inclined line of three motifs doubles in the top part.

5. The inclined line of three motifs is repeated in the bottom part. This way the complete floral design is obtained.

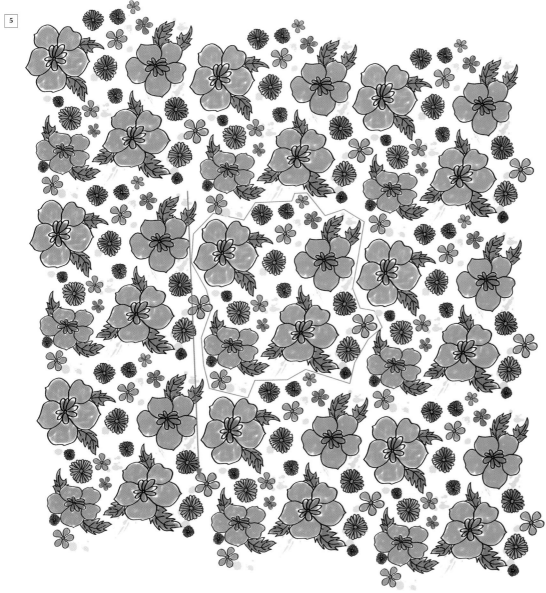

TECHNIQUES

Either through hand methods or through the use of digital technologies, designers have a great variety of techniques that they can use to place their designs on the fabric. In fact, any image, either an illustration or a photograph, can be printed on material through some specific procedure. Note, the results obtained will always be different from the visual point of view.

One of the most common techniques is screenprinting, a technique especially recommended for flat or plotted colours. This method of printing offers very different qualities with respect to the effects of colour and textures.

In turn, embroidery, with its great quantity of variants in threads and techniques, is another of the most commonly used techniques. It can be done manually or by machine. In the latter case, a computer program carries out a series of actions predetermined according to the illustration defined by the designer.

The other most often used technique is digital printing, which transfers the information to the printer for a jet of ink (*inkjet*) to recreate every type of image with great definition. The advantage of the digital process over the traditional one is that it allows passing directly from the design to the printing, without having to prepare screens and *shablones*. This last procedure is the one most used in *rapport* printing. The technique that is selected depends on the effect that the designer is looking for. Frequently the combination of different techniques offers the best results.

1-2. Screenprinting and the embroidery of sequins on silk *chiffon* are part of the same print and their development.

1

2

3. Original illustration with motifs of animals before the printing on final garment. By Miriam Ocáriz. Collection Spring-Summer 2008.

1

2

1. Original hand drawing rendered by linoleum on paper.

2. Lithograph on paper.

3. Manipulated digital image.

4. Handkerchief in silk chiffon, digital impression. By Javier Nanclares.

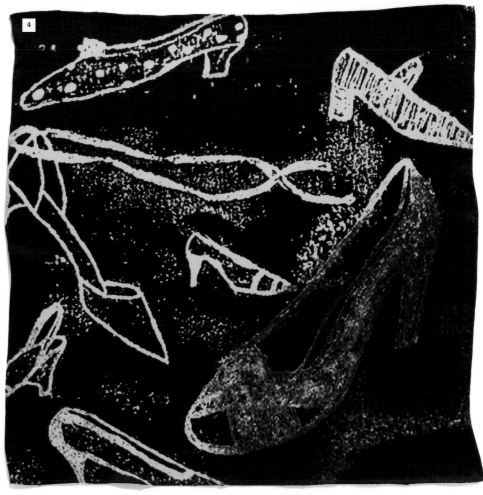

APPLICATION OF THE DESIGNS ONTO THE FABRIC
the final result

THE RAW MATERIAL

Either to obtain the best results on the textiles selected by the customer or to highlight the printing, the designer must have an in-depth knowledge of the raw materials. At present, the continuous research on new materials and the demands of the market make the textile industry one of the most dynamic and changing sectors. The most important lines of innovation are in the new fibres, membranes, processes and treatments, in which the biotechnology and the nanotechnology provide functional properties to the textile materials.

Besides the technical characteristics of the fabrics, designers must pay attention to the trends that appear in the sector of the market that their creations are destined for. For example, the increasing consciousness of the need to take care of the environment makes more designers and brands decide to use sustainable fabrics in their dressmaking.

The names of the fabrics indicate the method used to intertwine the threads and not the fibre that they contain. At first, some fabrics were only associated to the fibre that was used, as happened with taffeta or satin – made of silk, twill – a crossed fabric limited in the past to wool – or denim, that originally was only made of cotton. Today manufacturers produce taffeta from nylon, satin from cotton, twill from silk and denim from mixed fibres.

The common fabric – called smooth or taffeta fabric – is composed of two perpendicular series of threads, the warp that goes in a longitudinal direction, and the weft that goes in a transverse direction, in which each of their units receives the name of the last.

Other variations of the smooth fabric are the intermeshing or the fluted one. The crossed fabric, in turn, is characterised by the very marked diagonal lines caused by the intertwining of two threads of the warp with a thread of the weft in alternate rows. This effect can be observed in fabrics such as twill, gabardine or denim.

Satins have a texture denser than the crossed fabrics, but their main characteristic is their smoothness and endurance. The soft surface of satin is achieved by passing the threads of the warp over some threads of the weft with a minimum intertwining; the reflection of the light on the free threads produces its characteristic shine. The best known of these are the crepe satin, the silk satin and damask.

The harness and *jacquard* systems are used to manufacture materials with drawings on them such as brocades, whereas the fabrics with a pile, such as velvet, felt, corduroy and plush, are fabricated combining the smooth fabric with the use of wires that lift additional threads from the weft or the warp and form loops in the fabric. In plush, the loops are not cut, whereas with velvet they are.

There are also the textiles that are not woven, whose structure is achieved by joining or intertwining the fibres with mechanical, chemical or thermal methods, using solvents or combining the previous methods.

The appearance of the prints is different depending on the fibre, the weft and the finishing of the fabric. The same drawing on a light gauze of fine and transparent thread will acquire a different appearance on an opaque fabric of thicker texture and brightness, such as satin. Even if both fabrics are carried out in silk and they both have been printed with the same procedure and colouring, the effect will be different when using bases with different transparency, texture and brightness. Because of that, it is very important to recognise textile fibres and the way in which they will affect the printing and influence the final result. The chart on page 82 lists the different fibres with which the industry works.

The same print has been applied to garments of different materials: silk knit (), gauze () and satin ().

Initially, any fabric will be suitable for decoration by printing or applique and embroidery. Their composition does not have to be a problem when they merely serve as a base for the initial designs. However, the correct choice of the fabric can be important later on, depending on the final effect which the designer wants to obtain.

For more complex handwork such as batik, cotton or silk is generally used. To paint manually, the most popular technique is paint on silk, but it is also common to use other materials and techniques to obtain very different and creative work.

Screenprinting, because it is a superficial application, the same as sewing, embroidery and applique, is suitable for use on all the materials. Knitwear and jerseys, in turn, can be used for *transfers* or printing, as the inks are elastic nowadays and better penetrate into the fabric. Only in the case of the sublimation or the *devoré* technique is there a need to use a fabric with a percentage of polyester.

4. Original drawing for a print from the firm Miriam Ocáriz. Collection Fall-Winter 2008-2009.

5. The weight and the texture of the fabric define new dimensions in the prints.

5

4

THE FIBRES

The fibres that come from natural sources can be of a vegetable nature (composed of cellulose) or animal (composed of proteins).

The chemical fibres, in turn, can be artificial fibres, made from the transformation of natural polymers such as cellulose, or synthetic fibres, manufactured from polymers obtained industrially from derivatives of oil.

1. Presentation of the selection of fabrics with the prototypes of garments, from the collection of Syngman Cucala.

2. Applied on a fabric of brilliant fibres. In it the colours of this design stand out in a special way (WGSN).

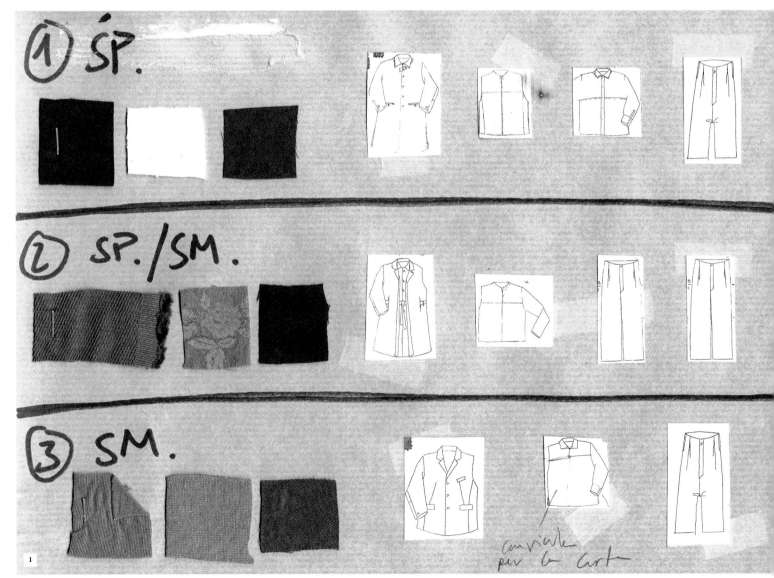

1

GENEALOGY OF THE FIBRES

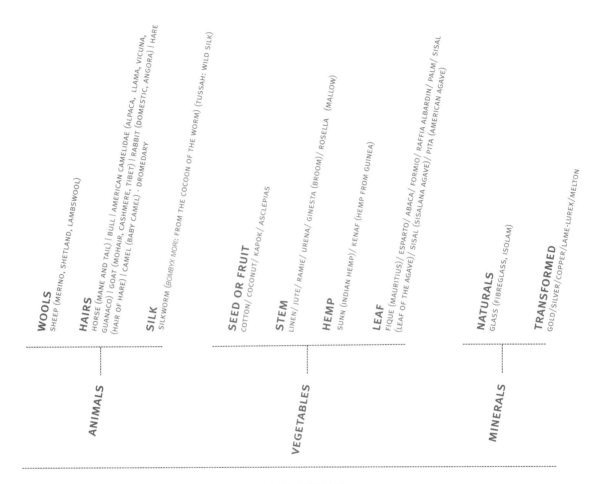

WOOLS
SHEEP (MERINO, SHETLAND, LAMBSWOOL)

HAIRS
HORSE (MANE AND TAIL) | BULL | AMERICAN CAMELIDAE (ALPACA, LLAMA, VICUNA, GUANACO) | GOAT (MOHAIR, CASHMERE, TIBET) | RABBIT (DOMESTIC, ANGORA) | HARE (HAIR OF HARE) | CAMEL (BABY CAMEL) - DROMEDARY

SILK
SILKWORM (*BOMBYX MORI*: FROM THE COCOON OF THE WORM) (*TUSSAH*: WILD SILK)

ANIMALS

SEED OR FRUIT
COTTON / COCONUT / KAPOK / ASCLEPIAS

STEM
LINEN / JUTE / RAMIE / URENA / GINESTA (BROOM) / ROSELLA (MALLOW)

HEMP
SUNN (INDIAN HEMP) / KENAF (HEMP FROM GUINEA)

LEAF
FIQUE (MAURITIUS) / ESPARTO / ABACA / FORMIO / RAFFIA ALBARDIN / PALM / SISAL (LEAF OF THE AGAVE) / SISAL (SISALANA AGAVE) / PITA (AMERICAN AGAVE)

VEGETABLES

NATURALS
GLASS (FIBREGLASS, ISOLAM)

TRANSFORMED
GOLD / SILVER / COPPER / LAME - LUREX / MELTON

MINERALS

NATURAL FIBRES

(1-2) PROTEINS (VEGETABLE OR ANIMAL ALBUMIN)
CASEIN (MERINOVA, FROM THE CASEIN OF MILK)/ LEGUMES (ARDIL, PEANUT, VICARA, CORN, SOY, SOY GRAINS)

(1) CELLULOSE (REGENERATED/MODIFIED)
VISCOSE (RAYON, VISCOSE, FIBRANA RAYON, VISCOSILLA, CUPROAMONIACALCUMPRAMA, RAYON TO COPPER, RAYON CUPRO)/ PAPER (WITH SODA OR SULPHITE)/ ESTERS OF CELLULOSE (DIACETATE-DICEL TRIACETATE-ARNEL TRICEL, TRILAN, TRIACETATE OF CELLULOSE)/ ACETATE (CELLULOSE ACETATE-RAYON ACETATE)

(1) ALGINIC
ALGINATES/ SEAWEEDS

(1) RUBBER AND GUM
GUM (FROM EXTRUDED LATEX (ROUND SECTION) OR FROM THE LEAVES (SQUARE SECTION)

CHLOROFIBRES
OF POLYVINYL (RHOVYL-MOVYL)/ OF POLYVILIDENO SARAN)

POLYAMIDES
NAILON 6 (PERLON, ENKALON)/ NAILON 6,6 (NYLON)/ NAILON II (RILSAN)/ NAILON HT (NOMEX)

POLYESTER
TERGAL/ TERLENKA

ACRYLIC
PURE (OURON, DRALON, LEACRIL, COURTELLE)/ MODIFIED (DYNEL)

OIL-BASED
POLYETHYLENE/ POLYPROPYLENE (MERCLON)

VINYL
ALCOHOL OF POLYVINYL (KURALON)

POLYURETHANE
LYCRA/ SPANDEX

FLUOROCARBONS
TEFLON

ARTIFICIAL
(FOR DISSOLUTION)
NATURAL POLYMERS
OF VEGETABLE (1) OR
ANIMAL (2)
ORIGIN

SYNTHETIC
(FOR REACTION)
SYNTHETIC POLYMERS

CHEMICAL FIBRES

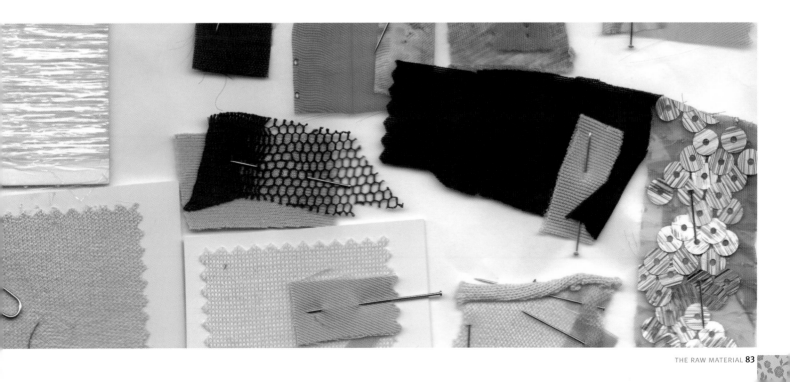

SPINNING

The fibres are processed through spinning to convert them into what will be used to weave, to sew and to embroider. The industrial technique of spinning is complex and it changes with the constant technological advances. It is adapted with great speed to the trends and demands of the market with respect to colouring, quality and finishes.

1-2-3. Prototypes of embroidery on fabrics of silk gauze and welded lattice, with embroidered wools. By María José Lleonar for the firm Simorra.

4-5-6-7. Four models with different printed dresses. Collection Fall-Winter 2006/2007. By Josep Font.

1

2

3

5

7

THE FABRICS

From the technical point of view, fabric is the name given to the material obtained in the form of a sheet more or less resistant, elastic and flexible, through the crossing and linking of two series of threads, one longitudinal and another transversal.

It is composed of a warp, which are the threads that go in longitudinal direction (thread) and a weft that are the threads that are intertwined in transverse direction (last). Depending on its structure they are classified as fabrics of plane or of sunk type, knitwear and fabrics that are not woven.

- **THE FABRICS OF THE PLANE OR OF THE SUNK TYPE**

These types of fabrics are defined in part from the method of construction:

  ▸ **SATIN** is woven so that the warp remains above the weft, or vice versa. This characteristic creates a soft, smooth and shining aspect to the front of the fabric and a matt back.

  ▸ **TAFFETA** presents a cross that is simpler and with a similar thickness of the threads. The thread of the warp and that of the weft passes in alternatively. An equally thick and smooth fabric is obtained on both sides, and there is not a front and back.

  ▸ **SERGE** presents a gradual structure with an oblique arrangement. The fabric has a face and a back, and is characterised by being quite strong. The fabric most characteristic of this technique is denim.

- **KNITWEAR**

They are the fabrics that are formed with at least a thread that is intertwined to itself. Hand knitting is done with needles: one does the knitting and the other one holds the fabric that is continually formed. From this technique derives knitting with machinery, where the material is built by intertwining loops of lines of thread in transverse and longitudinal directions. This composition is the one that provides the fabric with its characteristic elasticity. At the horizontal rows it designates the weft last and to the verticals, columns. In this case, the texture and the drawing are obtained through the use of several needles, threads, colours or the selection of different knitwear. Designs in knitted goods are also achieved by embroidery and the technique of screenprinting.

- **WELDED LATTICES**

Fabrics with metallic yarns are continually in fashion. Originally they came from threads of gold or silver, although at present the materials that are more commonly used are steel, aluminum, iron, nickel or alloys with cobalt. They can be of sunk type as well as of knitting.

- **THE WOVEN FABRICS THAT ARE NOT WOVEN**

This genre of fabrics that are not woven are also used in fashion, for sport footwear, linings, cushion fillings and accessories. Generally they are strong and resistant, and because of their construction they do not fray nor break easily. These fabrics are obtained by compressing fibres and then applying heat, friction or chemical products. One of the best known is felt. There are also the products created by DuPont, one of the more prestigious manufacturers in the development of this type of material.

- **SKIN AND LEATHER**

Thanks to the beauty of their fur, many animals are bred in farms to use their skins in fashion. For the textile designer, this is a very interesting resource, since the skins can be dyed with drawings, cut and manipulated with ornaments and embroidery.

Besides, strips of skin can be woven creating new textures and bits of skin can be included in collages. Leather can also generate a great number of effects when treated with dyes, textures and cutbacks, creating patent leathers and fantastic imitations of exotic skins, such as that of snake or crocodile. The use of animal skin today is very much a controversial subject. Nowadays this industry is totally legislated, therefore the animals destined for fashion are reared and killed under specific conditions.

- **PLASTICS**

Plastics are not natural products. They are obtained through different chemical processes to which an additive is incorporated. The results are called polymers. These fibres constitute the basis of plasticised fabrics, which are generally used in the design of rain or fantasy wear.

1-2-3. Print to be applied on flexible fabrics that adapt to the form of the body. From Lisa Italia. Collection Winter 2008.

4-5. Samples of vinyls (pvc) with colours, textures and prints.

6. Samples of skins with fur (astrakhan, ermine, mink, mouton) and imitation leathers with texture of snake and embossed floral print.

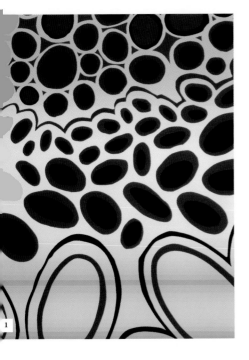

1

2

3

4

5

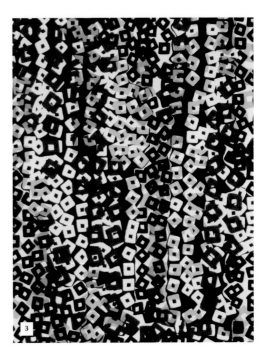

6

TYPES OF FABRICS

Sight and touch are the best means for recognising the different types of textiles. Here are some of the most widely used among hundreds of different qualities, which vary and change constantly as the industry progresses. Still, they always conserve their title in reference to their traditional name.

ACETATE. Chemical silk (artificial fibre), which is obtained from cellulose acetate, founded in Germany in 1869. Since 1920 this fibre has been used in the manufacture of lingerie, blouses, dresses and knitwear, as well as other garments requiring light and delicate fabrics. It is strong and easy to maintain, with no shrinking, wrinkling or fading. Washed under 104° F (40° C) and dried in the shade.

ALPACA. Material made of woven fibres of alpaca wool, used especially in making of men's clothing.

BATISTE. Named in honour of its creator Baptiste Cambray (a 13th-century French weaver). The batiste is a very fine fabric of linen or cotton, bleached in part, slightly prepared and hot-pressed. It is used for pocket handkerchiefs, dresses and shirts.

BROCADE. Sumptuous silk fabric made on a *jacquard* loom. Threads of gold or silver form part of the fabric (no embroidery), with relief as well as drawings of floral and arabesque motifs. It is used mainly in church ornaments and gowns.

CHIFFON. Fabric of silk or a synthetic fibre, very light and brilliant (with the appearance of gauze), woven with light fibres, but with twisted thread.

CHINTZ. Fabric originating in India, made of shiny cotton, and printed in bright colours.

CALICO. From Calicut, the city in India from which it was first imported. An inexpensive, plain white unprinted cotton cloth.

CORDUROY. From the Latin *pannus*, linen. It's the velvet weft. The warp and weft form the base fabric and the other weft, the rough cut, shapes the characteristic feel of this fabric. Usually woven of cotton, but also with rayon. Corduroy can also be smooth, square and adorned. Traditionally, the corduroy of brown or black colour was the typical fabric of peasants. Today, manufactured in all colours and a wide variety of thicknesses, it also comes in a variety of weights.

COTELINE. Ribbed fabric made of wool or cotton. Used formerly for suits, jackets, blazers and coats.

COTTON. Vegetable fibre that is separated from the seeds (which it covers) of the cotton plant. The quality of cotton depends on its fineness, purity, brilliance and, above all, the length of the fibre; the older it is, the thinner, more resistant and more regular is the thread that is produced. Linens and bedding are made from short cotton fibre cuts. Long fibres are used for batiste fabrics, poplin and damask. This fibre is highly absorbent, resistant to heat, washable, and not susceptible to moths. It is not compressable nor does it accrue static electricity. Untreated, it is used to make wadding.

CREPE OR CRÊPE. Fabrics made of silk, linen and cotton which have a wrinkly surface.

CRÊPE GEORGETTE. Fabric very lightweight and transparent, matt and soft to the touch.

CRESPON. Thin and wrinkled fabric that is produced by twisting many of the warp and weft threads. It is made in wool, silk, cotton, rayon, linen, and also in combinations. Usually it is printed and used a lot in women's clothing.

CRETONNE. Cotton fabric printed in colours, on which flowers are the typical pattern. It is a strong fabric that is used mainly for curtains and upholstery.

DAMASK. Originally a figured fabric of silk or linen with designs worked into fabric, showing a shiny pattern on one side and the same inverted design on the other. Fabrics of cotton, rayon, wool or blends in a jacquard-style fabric are also known as damask.

DENIM. It is the fabric of all cowboy fashion. It entered the fashion world in the 1940s. It is a twilled fabric, made of cotton, very resistant, easy to wash and very hard-wearing.

FELT. Textile product obtained without weaving. Manufactured by making use of the properties of certain fibres – especially wool – to interlace and cling together. These properties are encouraged by the friction of the fibres in a water-based medium with pressure and heat.

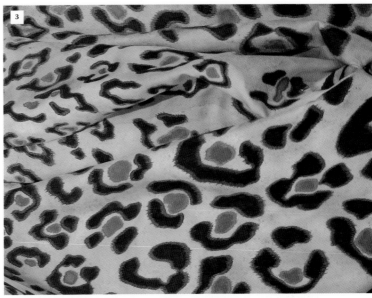

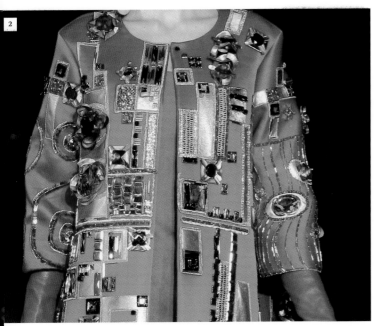

1. Embroidery with silk threads on Shantung of natural silk of the collection by the designer Manuel Albarrán.

2. Prints with applications of stones and metallic pieces. By Christian Dior. Collection Spring-Summer 2008.

3. Print of leopard on silk. By Christian Dior.

FLANNEL. Generic name for several woollen fabrics that have in common a simple or cross weft. They are smooth to the touch because the finish is combed on one side. When made with thin threads of wool, it is used for coats and suits, and with cotton, raising one or both sides, for indoor clothing such as pajamas and shirts. Flannelette, which is a lighter and softer material, is always made of combed cotton.

GABARDINE. A closely woven twill fabric. It also often has artificial fibres and different thicknesses. Since 1902, gabardine is a trademark registered by the firm Burberry.

GAUZE. Probably from Arabic *Gazza*, silk, or from Gaza, a city in Palestine. A thin, lightly woven, transparent silk material used for transparent blouses, dresses and scarves. There is also a cotton gauze which has a very loose weave and is heavily treated.

GEORGETTE. Very fine and transparent crepe that is made from highly twisted threads.

GLACILLA. Fabric used in tests before using the original fabric.

GROSGRAIN. Special fabric for ribbons of silk, rayon or cotton, that is horizontally fluted.

GUIPURE. Thick lace and with a drawing with a background of ties or also thick thread.

JERSEY. Fine knitwear originally created on the island of Jersey (United Kingdom). Can be manufactured from various textile materials on warp or weft circular knitting machines or straight machines.

LAMÉ. French name (lamina) given to sumptuous fabrics that have fancy threads of gold or silver interwoven in them. It is used in dresses and ballgowns.

LINEN. A cloth made from flax fibre whose threads frequently have an irregularity of thickness. The fabric is fine and strong but it does not have easy-care properties.

LYCRA. Chemical fibre based on elastomers of polyurethane, manufactured exclusively by the firm Du Pont (Delaware, USA.). It is elastic, resistant to fire and to humidity and it holds its shape. It is an essential component of undergarments and a lot of sportswear. When it is mixed with other fabrics, it adds elasticity to the weave.

MADRAS. Cloth exported from India to the West for over a century. It is light, open fabric made of cotton, woven by hand, dyed with vegetable dyes and hand printed with patterns and motifs typical of their country of origin.

MATT. This term refers to many fabrics made of cotton or linen. In embroidery, it refers to when the weft is very visible and is regulated by positioning each point or cutting the openwork with precision (Hardanger). There are different sizes designated by a figure that corresponds to the number of weft threads per centimeter or per inch (2.54 centimetres).

MOHAIR. Fabric made from hair of the Angora goat or by mixing this with cotton, wool or silk. It always has a side of frayed hair.

MOIRE. (or Moara) Fabric usually of silk whose thick weft of silk, *schappe* or cotton make horizontal cords, also known as *fay*. It is referred to as watered silk because its main feature is the optical effect that occurs in the form of wavy reflections, or waters, which change according to the incidence of light shining on it.

MUSLIN. Fabric originally from Mussul (Iraq). It arrived in Western Europe in the 17th century and in the 18th century began to be manufactured in England and France. In the 1960s it was especially popular for dresses of the *hippie* fashion. It is a woven cotton which is lightweight, translucent and can range from soft to the touch to coarse.

ORGANDY. (ORGANDIE) Fabric made from cotton with very fine and regular threads. Two important features of organdy are its semi-transparency and rigidity, which reappear when ironing the fabric after washing. It is a fine, thin muslin.

PERCALE. (from the Persian *pargale*) a smooth, closely woven lightweight material usually made of cotton. Similar to cretonne but of a better, finer and higher density. Can be bleached, dyed in part or, more generally, printed. Frequently used for bed linens.

PIQUÉ. From the French word, piquér. Stiff corded fabric generally woven from cotton that has geometric patterns on it. More commonly it is made of materials with two sides or double-sided fabric, leading to drawings that are more or less geometrical in relief. The material is often bleached, although it is sometimes dyed in light colours.

1. Taffeta of silk with hand embroidery.

2. Embroidery, with metallic threads and applique, on silk taffeta. By Christian Dior. Collection Spring-Summer 2008.

3. Silk chiffon dress with a floral print. Spring-summer 2009 (Première Vision Paris.)

4. Silk taffeta dress with geometrical motifs and sequins embroidered on it. By Christian Dior. Spring-Summer 2008.

PLUSH. From the old German *felbel*, it is a type of velvet though it has a longer and more open pile than ordinary velvet. Generally the pile is made of wool or cotton, made up by the warp threads. It's called plush long hair when the pile is 0.4 inches (1 cm) in length.

POPLIN. Strong fabric that was first manufactured in Avignon when this city was the papal seat. It could be that its name derives from that time. Currently poplin is made in combed and mercerised cotton, or in blends of cotton, silk, wool and artificial and synthetic fibres. It is a very durable material and is used especially for shirts and blouses.

SATIN. Name that might have the same Latin origin of silk or be originally from a town in China where a very thick and shining fabric of silk was woven. Nowadays it is also made from rayon, the fabric often replacing silk. It is a luxury fabric that is often used for wedding gowns, formal dresses or nightwear.

SILK SATIN. Silk fabric with warp of silk or mercerised cotton and weft of other fibres, always with a smooth and lustrous surface, for the effect of a silk-like material.

Hard-wearing twilled worsted fabric.

SHANTUNG. Fabric formerly made with greige silk that was spun in Shantung (China). It is now also made of cotton and rayon. It is also known as a fabric of wild silk with varying thicknesses presented in the form of flames.

SPANDEX. Fabric of the fibre of the same name. It is very elastic; used for stockings, corsetry and swimwear.

TAFFETA. From the Persian tâftah, meaning spinning, and täfteh, meaning brilliant. Thick fabric made of fine threads of silk or slightly stiff cotton. It has a crisp feel like silk and an iridescent appearance.

VELVET. Fabric with a short, thick and perpendicular pile. Initially made of silk and later of rayon this fabric was often associated with luxury.

TULLE. First appeared in Tulle (France) in the mid-18th century. Originally done by hand, it is a stiffened, sheer net made of silk or cotton. Today it is made on special looms.

TWEED. Woven wool fabric of bulky and strong appearance originally produced by hand in homes in southern Scotland. Today this name refers to tweeds manufactured on the loom, usually of wool though sometimes with a bit of cotton added in.

VELOUR. From the French word which meaning velvet. Currently known by this name are items with a surface imitating silk velvet knitted from synthetic fibres. It is used for trim and decoration.

VICHY. From the French *vichy*, it is a fine cotton fabric with threads of bright and solid colours forming simple drawings (lists and tables). Used for gowns for women, common linen and shirts for men.

WAXED. Ribbon or strong fabric with a glossy finish wax.

1-2. Original design applied to both silk gauze and satin silk, which makes evident the difference in transparency and brightness obtained on each surface. From SIMORRA.

1

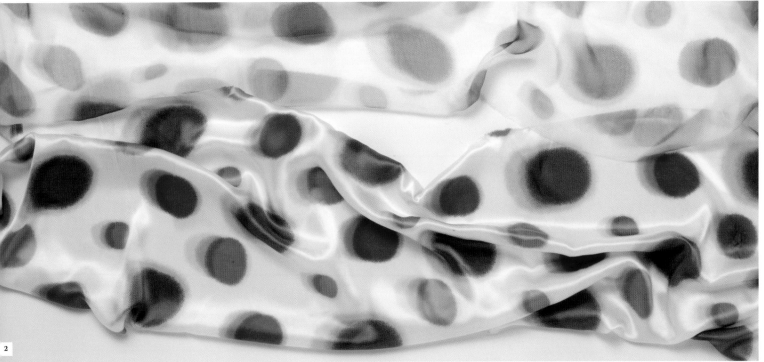

2

1-2. Floral designs on muslin. From the firm Miriam Ocáriz.

DYES, VARNISHES AND PIGMENTS

Dye is a pigmented substance with a density that can range from liquid to viscose. Its components are the pigment – or dye – known as colouring, the binding also called the vehicle, which is the heavy medium in which the pigment is dispersed; and other additives such as stabilisers, solvents and softeners. The dyes most frequently used are:

PLASTISOL OR ACRYLIC VARNISHES. They are known for their shininess and elasticity. They are also very durable and resistant to washing.

BLEACHES. Ideal for whitening natural fabrics, to discolour already dyed fabrics or to obtain the effects of being cleaned with bleach and being aged.

BASE COLOURS. They are applied on dark fabrics.

GLUE. Self-adhesive plastisol which can be used in achieving various effects, for example: crimson velvet, caviar (gluing small beads), glitter, metallic, etc.

INKS WITH SPECIAL EFFECTS. Metallised (gold, silver, bronze, copper), luminous or aged, glitter and pearly.

VARNISHES FOR FLOCKING. Dyes suitable for producing a raised, velvety surface.

DYES OF HIGH DENSITY. Used for prints requiring high relief.

NATURAL DYES AND ORGANIC PIGMENT. They are extracted from plants, animals and minerals. Currently with all the interest in green issues, there is renewed interest in their use.

WATER-BASED DYES. There are different variants for natural, mixed or synthetic blend fabrics. They are suitable for plain fabrics.

1. Cans of paint with their colour reference numbers of in a screenprinting workshop.

2. Although the workshops have computer programs to decide on the composition of various colours, frequently they resort to mixing the colours by hand with a special scale.

3. Drawing prepared in layers for the screenprinting workshop. The textile designer indicates the colours that compose the drawing: the first is the background colour (that of the fabric), and for the other five a layer of colour is applied to each. The workshop should prepare therefore, five dyes or varnishes with the colour desired, and five screens, one for each colour.

4. A blank silk-screen, formed by a frame with a fabric, on which an emulsion will applied, tautly stretched over it. Originally, these screens were made of silk. Today there are other, stronger materials that allow reuse of the screens.

5. Ultraviolet light used in the the screenprinting process. Once the emulsion is applied to the screen (see pp. 102), the screen is subjected to a light which fixes the design onto the screen.

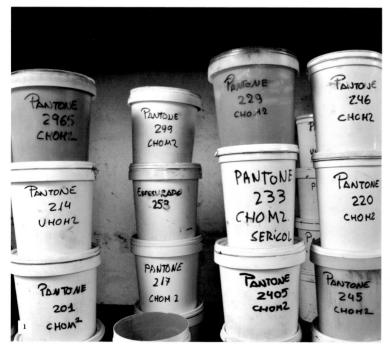

 Col 1: ground
Col. 210 milky petrol

 **Col 2: softhand print**
Col. 920 anthra

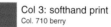 **Col 3: softhand print**
Col. 710 berry

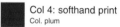 **Col 4: softhand print**
Col. plum

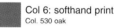 **Col 5: softhand print**
Col. sporty green

 Col 6: softhand print
Col. 530 oak

• Crystals

FINAL PRINTING PROCESSES

Printing is the process by which the colouration of a fabric according to the preconceived profiles or drawings is finally carried out. In this process, the colouring material is intimately linked to the fabric.

In the final process of bringing the designs to the fabric there are often several different techniques that come together to ensure that the result is true to what the designer intended.

For example, you may find the same garment on which various printing techniques have been applied with differing effects, and that includes adding some work of industrial or hand embroidery.

The use of multiple techniques is possible by technological advances that constantly generate new possibilities for printing and embroidery, as well as offering a wide range of methods by which to manipulate the fabric.

1

2

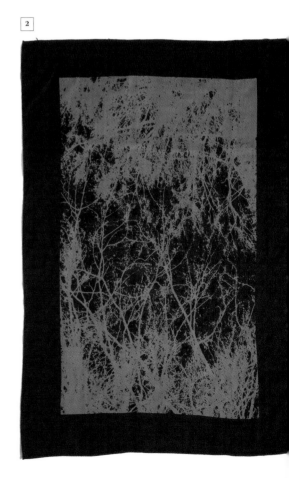

1. Screenprinting in a single colour on red silk. By Javier Nanclares.

2. Printing a single colour ink – pink – on green silk.

3. Fabric decorated with a combination of screenprinting and industrial embroidery with threads of various colours and the application of sequins.

4. Printed paper for which one needs ten silk-screens to achieve that number of colours. From the firm Lissa Italia.

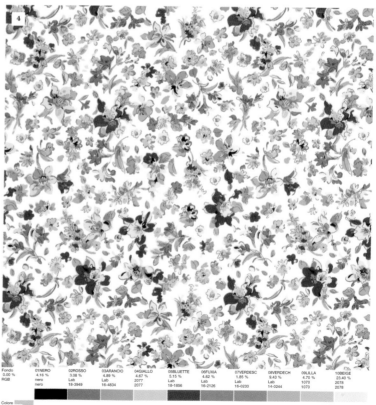

Fondo 0.00 % RGB	01NERO 4.16 % nero nero	02ROSSO 3.08 % Lab 18-3949	03ARANCIO 4.89 % Lab 2077	04GIALLO 4.67 % Lab 2077	05BLUETTE 5.15 % Lab 18-1856	06FUXIA 4.62 % Lab 16-2126	07VERDESC 1.85 % Lab 16-0233	08VERDECH 9.43 % Lab 14-0244	09LILLA 4.70 % 1070 1070	10BEIGE 23.40 % 2078 2078

Colore
Non stampa

Lisa Spa - Disegno A0960 Variante: DB1
Data 14/03/2008

SCREENPRINTING

One printing technique that is frequently used is serigraphy or printing with a screen. This consists of separating the drawing to be transferred to the fabric into different layers that correspond to each of the colours that the design contains. For each of these layers there is a stencil with the picture you want to appear on the black opaque screen. Then the design is placed on the rectangular frame, of wood or metal, which holds the screen – a special taut fabric to which emulsion has already been applied. The light fixes the emulsion and leaves free the mesh areas on which the drawing is found which are the areas that will need to be inked. After removing the screen, it is washed to remove the emulsion in areas where the picture appears. The emulsion will cover the areas where there will be no image, leaving free the area in which you want to print the colour.

This process is repeated using a screen for each colour to be printed. In this way, the design is transferred to the fabric by pressing the ink through each screen and onto the fabric below. When the screenprinting is done manually it is a person who runs the press and pushes the squeegee to press the ink onto the fabric below. In a similar manner when the process is done industrially, the fabric goes along a conveyor belt and the screens, each with a part of the design, are placed on the fabric and a mechanical arm spreads the ink over the screen.

Another method of screenprinting involves first dyeing the fabric and then printing the picture with a corrosive paste that will remove the colour. Generally, this is done on dark backgrounds.

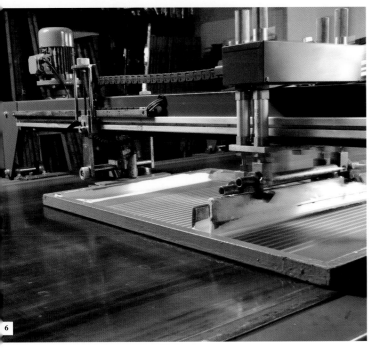

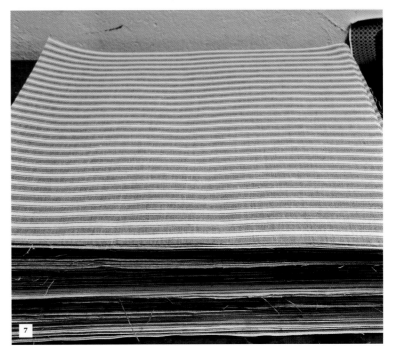

Different stages of industrial screenprinting in a specialised workshop.

4. Screen with a design of simple lines.

5. Industrial process machine with several screens that requires a man to place and remove the fabric. The screen is larger than the fabric in order to perform a complete printing.

6. The machine lowers the screen onto the fabric, applying the emulsion and using a spatula or squeegee to distribute the colour.

7. Stacked printed fabrics.

Silk-screen for the colour blue. It rks as a negative image. The screen th the drawing that will appear as ck opaque so that no light reaches the reen.

The rear view of a completed screen ady to be printed for a single colour. hen the colour is applied with a ueegee on the screen, the pigment netrates through the screen marking e drawing on the fabric below.

Sample of a black background printed th five colours: yellow, white, green, d and blue. The dark background has quired the use of opaque plastisols in der to obtain the vivid and bright lours. These, in turn, are sensitive to e touch because they generate a thick vering of paint.

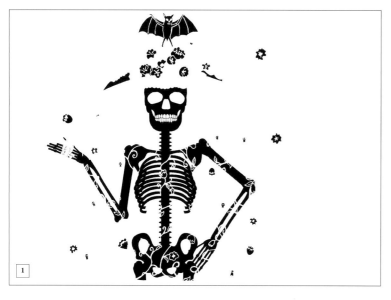

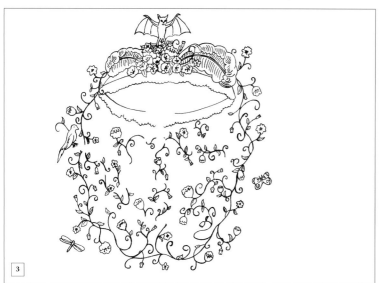

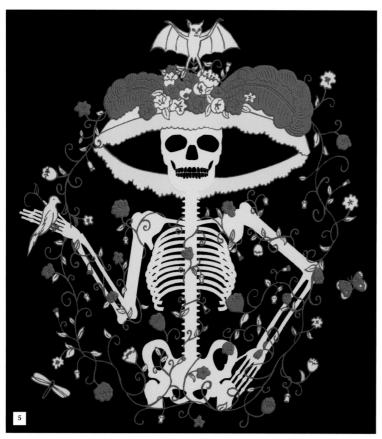

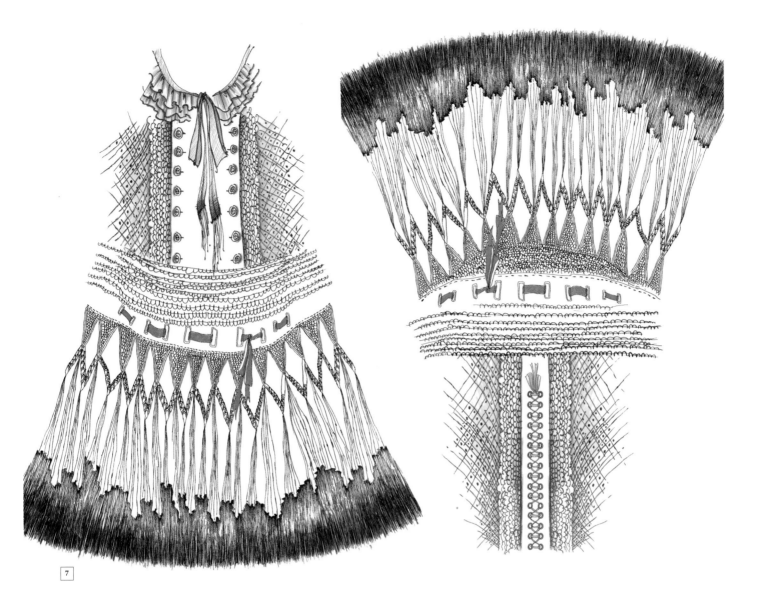

1-2-3-4. Screens for each of the four colours in the drawing.

5. Positional design of four colours on black background. From the firm Mátala Mamá.

6. The design applied on dress. From the firm Mátala Mamá.

7-8. The design on this garment takes up its complete surface, taking into account that the ribbon is positional. The result of the screenprinting on the garment is shown on page 49. From the firm Miriam Ocáriz.

DEVORÉ

The relief effect known as *devoré* is also obtained through a screenprinting process when printing with known chemicals such as a *devoré* paste on a fabric with fibres from different groups. The *devoré* paste is an ink that in its composition destroys cotton. For example, in a garment with a blend of cotton and polyester, the cotton becomes detached in the area that had been previously printed, and the polyester remains, creating a relief effect. If the portion of cotton that composes the fabric is greater than that of polyester, the effect is more noticeable.

1. Printed with *devoré* effect, a result of the subtraction of the velvet cotton in specific areas that leave in evidence the polyester base.

2. Drawing prepared for sending to the workshop where the printing will be carried out that will result in the *devoré*.

3. Design to carry out a false *devoré* on the women's T-shirts through printing with the tail and *transferring* to velvet. By Laura Fernandez.

Colour 1 ground	Colour 2 softhand print		
Col. 210 milky petrol	Col. 269 inky green		
Colour 3 softhand print	Cristals		
Col. 209 teal green			

DIGITAL PRINTING

Digital printing (offset, inkjet) is the great technological advance of recent years as far as reproduction of images. It is carried out with a large printer that has been prepared for transferring the design to a great variety of surfaces, among them the fabric. With this device it is possible to print any type of image, from the most complex of drawings up to a photograph, without limiting colours or effects. For this to happen, the designer must present the motif to be printed in a digital file format, preferably with extension .tiff or .eps. The result is of a definition and accuracy that gives the designer great creative freedom.

Thanks to this process the stencils, screens and other preliminaries usually necessary disappear.

Another of its great advantages is that it produces samples with great speed and facilitates the control of the process through immediate corrections, without wasting time nor money. Digital printing does not waste ink and that's why it is a clean and ecological method to use. This technique is constantly evolving, so the industry annually organises fairs in different cities around the world at which to show the new machinery and the possibilities for printing with them. These are unmissable events for everyone who needs to be up to date on the latest innovations and who wants to take most advantage of them.

1. Silk gauze with printed digitally.
From the firm Lissa Italia.

1

2

3

2-3-4-5. Photographic effects printed digitally on this collection of silk handkerchiefs. By Javier Nanclares.

4

5

01VIOLASC	01VIOLACH	03FUXIA	04ARANCIO	05GIALLO	06TURCHESESC	07TURCHESECH	08OCRASC	09OCRACH	10BEIGE
3.62 %	6.21 %	2.37 %	4.52 %	10.28 %	2.49 %	3.63 %	9.56 %	7.57 %	5.95 %
2042	2043	2044	1850	322	158	666	976	1723	669
2042	2043	2044	1850	322	158	666	976	1723	669

Colore
Non stampa

12Fondo
27.93 %
1114
1114

Digitally printed paper with a variety of colours. From the firm Lissa Italia.

EMBROIDERY

Embroidery is a needlework technique by which designs can be produced on textile fabrics.

Its application aims to both decorate the fabric as well reproduce a design. Embroidery appears on top of the material. Knitted fabrics also often incorporate in their construction additions such as pearls, woven glasses, sequins, gems, tapes and ribbons. Textile manufacturers use this technique to produce fabrics that often turn out to be exquisite works of craftsmanship. In some cases they highlight the properties of the fabric through brightness and textures, and in others they manipulate the fabric to make exciting surface shapes and forms. An example of this is the work of the British designer Anne Kyrö Quinn (see pag.184) who builds her textiles through height and textures, with an almost architectural vision.

TYPES OF EMBROIDERY

HEMSTITCH. Traditional trimming technique in which threads are pulled together in a group, creating a series of tiny bead-like openings and a hem.

CROSS-STITCH. A basic technique that consists of forming crosses by pulling a few threads through a fabric.

PALESTRINA STITCH. Also known as the Old English knot stitch. Rows of knots are placed together to form a textured surface.

CHAIN STITCH. This stitch resembles a crochet chain and its function is almost identical.

PARMA EMBROIDERY. Consists of a four-sided pattern, in same colour threads on a cheaply woven fabric.

LAGARTERA EMROIDERY. Type of very elaborate Spanish embroidery, which uses satin and double running stitches. There are two main variants: lagartera closed and open (sunk).

HARDANGER. Very difficult but exquisite Norwegian embroidery. It is stitched white on white and contains solid blocks of stitches contrasting with lacy open work.

ENHANCEMENT. Embroidery used to enhance designs or to provide eye-catching initials and logos.

RICHELIÉU EMBROIDERY. It consists in cutting away the fabric and and working over the edges with stitches such as the buttonhole stitch.

EMBROIDERY ON TULLE. Small decorative elements are mechanically applied to tulle.

SMOCKING. This is an embroidery stitch that is traditionally used on children's clothes. It produces a honeycomb-looking effect.

MANILA EMBROIDERY. The origin of this embroidery is in China. Very well-known for its application on the typical hand-embroidered Spanish shawls, which are called 'Manila shawls'. It is applied also to other garments, such as kimonos, cushions or pictures. Traditionally they were carried out in silk and were embroidered by hand with nature motifs and other characteristic Chinese designs.

An alternative option to hand done embroidery is the industrial option, which is done by machine. An example of this is the *transfer* of sequins, glass and applications with special effects, that they put on the fabric by thermobonding. The great advantage of industrial embroidery is the large number of garments that can be embroidered in a comparatively small time. However, it does lack the creative quality that a hand craftsman who likes experimenting with stitches could produce.

1. Prototype design by María José Lleonar for the firm Simorra.

2. Hand embroidery with cotton threads of various colours and with applications of stones. From the firm Ventures India.

3-4-5-6. Drawings and industrial prototypes with embroidery for enhancement (**4**) and in the Manila style (**6**). By María José Lleonar for the firm Simorra.

7-8. Specification sheets for embroidery to be done in an industrial embroidery workshop.

3

5

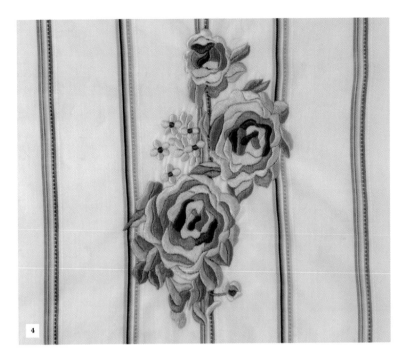

4

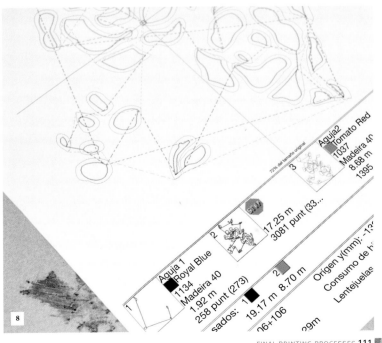

6

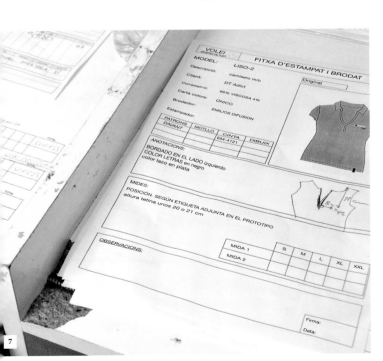

7

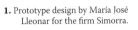

8

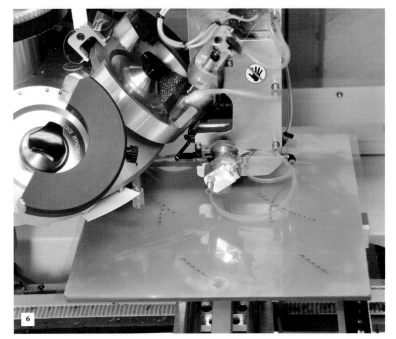

1-2. Industrial embroidery workshop in which embroidery is being worked onto a frame.

3. Industrial embroidery. From the firm Cadena.

4. Industrial machinery for application of embroidery and sequins.

5. Sample of fabric with embroidery and sequins, subsequent to the process of printing.

6. Machine that carries out *transfers* with applications.

7. Prototype of industrial chain stitch embroidery that combines two colours and two fabrics.

8. *Transfers* to be applied to the fabric by thermobonding.

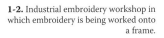

The alta costura allows embroiderers to present exquisite designs without loss of creativity or at an exorbitant cost. From the firm Christian Dior. Haut Couture Collection Winter 2008.

Hand embroidery carried out in India with silk, silver and gold threads, and the application of sequins and stones, on a base of fabric of silk for undergarments. By Manuel Albarrán.

MATERIAL FOR EMBROIDERING

Threads used in embroidery vary greatly in quality, thickness, and texture. There also come in a wide range of colours. Ornaments and applique can also be used in the embroidery. The threads that are used in this technique are the same ones that are used for the woven fabric, but especially used are the classics of cotton, silk, polyester, wool and linen, and even those of silver and gold are used with the different forms that are adopted in the art of stitching.

Likewise, there are combinations that generate new effects, such as the twist, composed of three twisted threads; the wavy thread which can be done in gold as well as in silver; another uses a thread of greater thickness; another effect is one that uses a thread with lateral notches, and finally there is one that can be presented curly, smooth, matt or shiny and in several thicknesses.

The most frequent ornaments are the pearls, the type of glass and crystal produced by Swarovski, sequins of several sizes and in chain, precious or imitation stones, fabrics, ribbons and tapes.

1-2-3-4-5. Embroideries with different threads on silk taffeta. From the firm Ventures India.

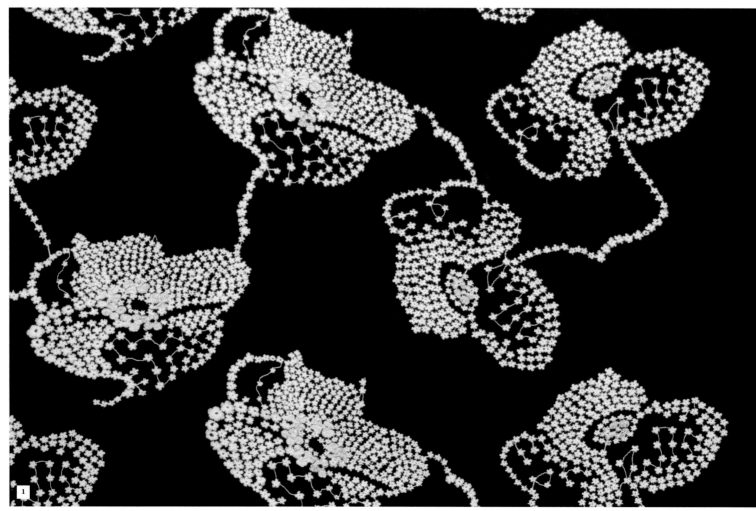

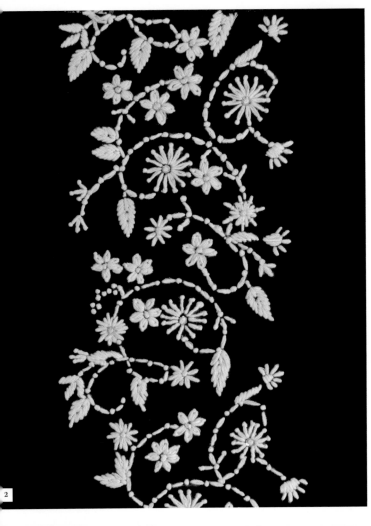

ROLLER PRINTING

This sytem was developed in the period when textile operations were first mechanised (from 1785). The technique consists of a cylinder or roller of cast iron and another of copper, engraved with the design, under which slides the fabric that is to be printed with successive applications of colour. These cylinders turn to a container from where they take up the colour. Because the cylinders are quite costly and because each can print one only colour, this system is almost never used today.

THERMOTRANSFERENCE OR SUBLIMATION

Printing through thermotransference is a procedure in which the designs are transferred to the fabric through heat and pressure through a paper especially printed by rotogravure, offset or screenprinting.

The fabric or garment is placed on a plastic frame and dampened in a special solution. The paper with the design is placed on the fabric, which remains taut on a frame, and then moistened in a special solution, and covered with a layer of silicon treated oilskin.

The set is treated with pressure and heat until the drawing is vaporised and the design is passed to the fabric. Through this method one obtains better penetration of the dye in the fabric, greater compatibility between design and printing, smaller industrial costs and less pollution. Nowadays this process is also carried out digitally.

1. Printing through thermotransference.

2. Design of complex composition, suitable to be carried out industrially with a system of rollers for a four-colour printing process. From the firm Basso & Brooke.

2

1. Traditional Indian blocks used for printing on textiles.

2. Linoleum blocks and materials used for printing.

3. Design printed with linoleum blocks.

BLOCK PRINTING

Printing with stamp pads is one of the oldest techniques. It consists of carving the surface of a hard material (such as wood, linoleum or rubber) to obtain an image in negative relief. The obtained stamp pad or block is then inked and applied through pressure onto leaving the designed image on the fabric. In 1834 printing with blocks became mechanised. The technique allowed their mass production with a variety of motifs and colours.

Traditionally, blocks for printing have been made in wood, although especially in Europe a great number were made of metal attached to a base of wood. The woods most suitable for the making of blocks are those that have a dense grain, the hard and resistant ones, such as box, beech or sycamore, among others.

The making of blocks or wooden stamps requires a very specialised aptitude in which the skill of carving the wood is the most important. Woodcutting is a complex discipline that requires not only a skill in handling tools but also a knowledge of wood grains and cross grains. The making of these blocks is a discipline that traditionally has been done by master craftsmen and is not much practised at present.

1

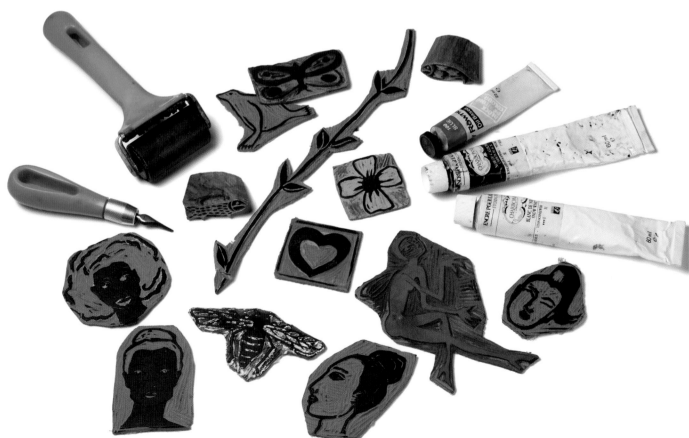

2

RESIST PRINTING

In these prints, the drawing is defined when one dyes a fabric previously treated so that the colour does not penetrate into specific areas, usually called 'resist'. The technique of batik is the well-known and simple version of this technique. In this case, the design is drawn with hot wax so that, when it solidifies, it works as an insulating layer. This way, when the fabric is dyed, the covered areas remain reserved or unprinted. The colours are worked from lighter to darker ones, covering new parts with wax and dyeing the design again until it is completed. At the end of the process, the wax is removed with a solvent or with heat.

Another common technique is *Shibori*, a Japanese term that is applied generically to differently used procedures for dyeing fabrics using resists. Unlike with batik, areas are not covered with wax, but through procedures of bundling, sewing, bending, rolling up, gathering, etc.

One of the most attractive features of this technique is that it implies a certain degree of unpredictability; while keeping within the general looked for effect, the results are always different.

The Western adaptation of the *shibori* is 'tie and dye', a technique in which a fabric that previously has been knotted or tied with threads is dyed.

Serti for its part – in French, to set – is the technique of printing on silk in which resists, generally gutta (material specifically for painting on silk) or a water-based one, are used to mark out the area that one desires to colour. The colour then appears in the interior of the drawing that has been marked with the resist.

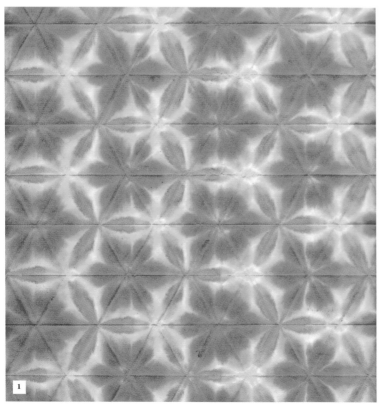

1. Japanese print done in the resist technique known as *shibori*.

2. Print done in the batik technique.

3. The tie and dye technique obtains a design by knotting the fabric to form the resist.

4. Japanese tie and dye print that was achieved by placing small seeds in the tied part of the fabric to form the resulting pattern.

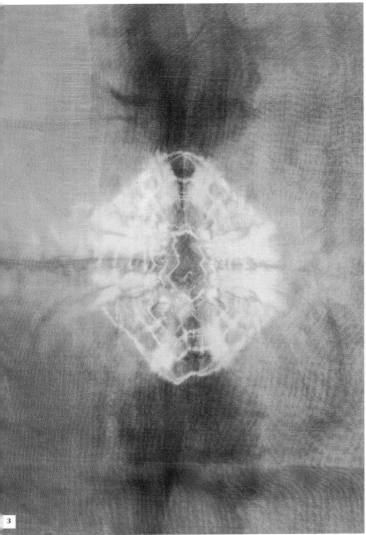

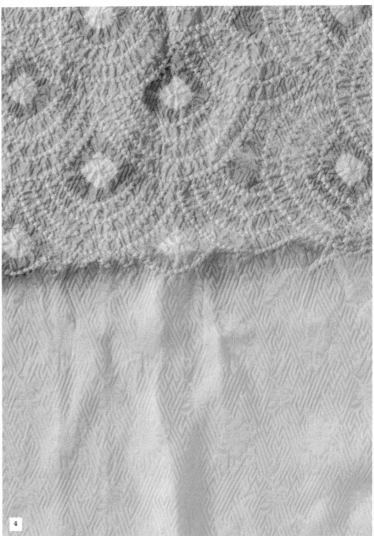

THE FINAL PRODUCT

Fabrics are the most obvious place to use printing. However, frequently textile designers choose to apply prints directly to a specific area of the garment (low collars, pockets, sleeves or T-shirts), on a handkerchief or scarf, on accessories (bags, belts, socks, gloves, etc.), on applications (patch or ornament) or the label.

Another factor that must be taken into account when considering the design, is the sector of the market to which the garment is directed. The shapes and colours of the motifs will be very different when they are applied to textiles for children, babies, men or women, clothes for parties, weddings and ceremonies, lingerie and bathing or sportswear. The designer has the option of specialising in a specific sector of the market, but the more versatile one is, the more possibilities for work will be presented to him or her.

Sometimes, the textile designer and the fashion designer do not have any contact. In these cases, the firm or fashion designer will buy the fabric with the already finished design at fairs or through the commercial textile companies.

However, on other occasions, both creative partners have a very direct relationship, working together up to the end, from the initial presentation of the product through to the final labelling.

Also common are the occasions when the textile designer receives a specific assignment from the fashion house, to carry out prints according to the concept of the collections that will be presented in each season.

1. The print composed by stains and irregular brushstrokes adds to the garment's feeling of looseness. From the firm Sharon Wauchob.

2. Print that simulates the woven tartan, done with a sequential geometrical design of lines of colours and varied proportions. From the firm Basso & Brooke.

3. Design composed of threads of different fibres and colours. From the firm Louis Feraud.

Designs inspired by the folklore of the countries of Eastern Europe. By Atelier Lzc for the firm Adieu Tristesse.

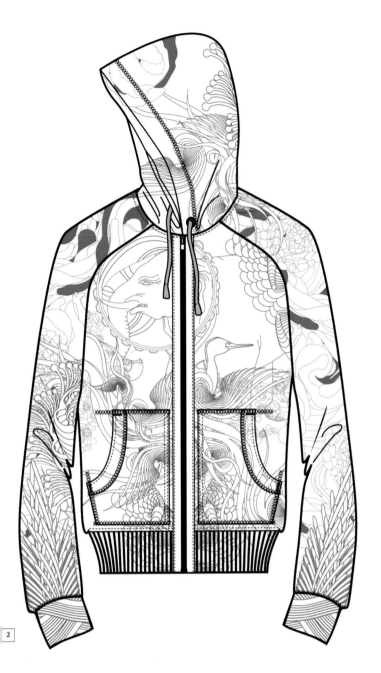

2

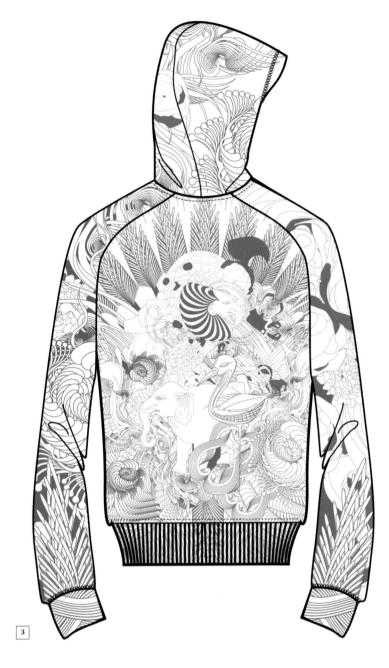

3

1. Technical drawing of the design entitled 'Elephant'. From the firm Artful Dodger.

2-3. Design 'Elephant', conceived for embroidery and printing, inspired by Indian iconography and applied to a line of streetwear. By Inocuo The Sign for the firm Artful Dodger.

4. Design 'Elephant' applied on a pullover. From the firm Artful Dodger.

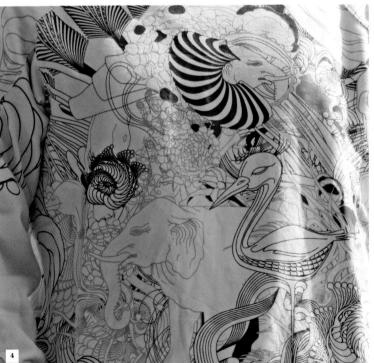

4

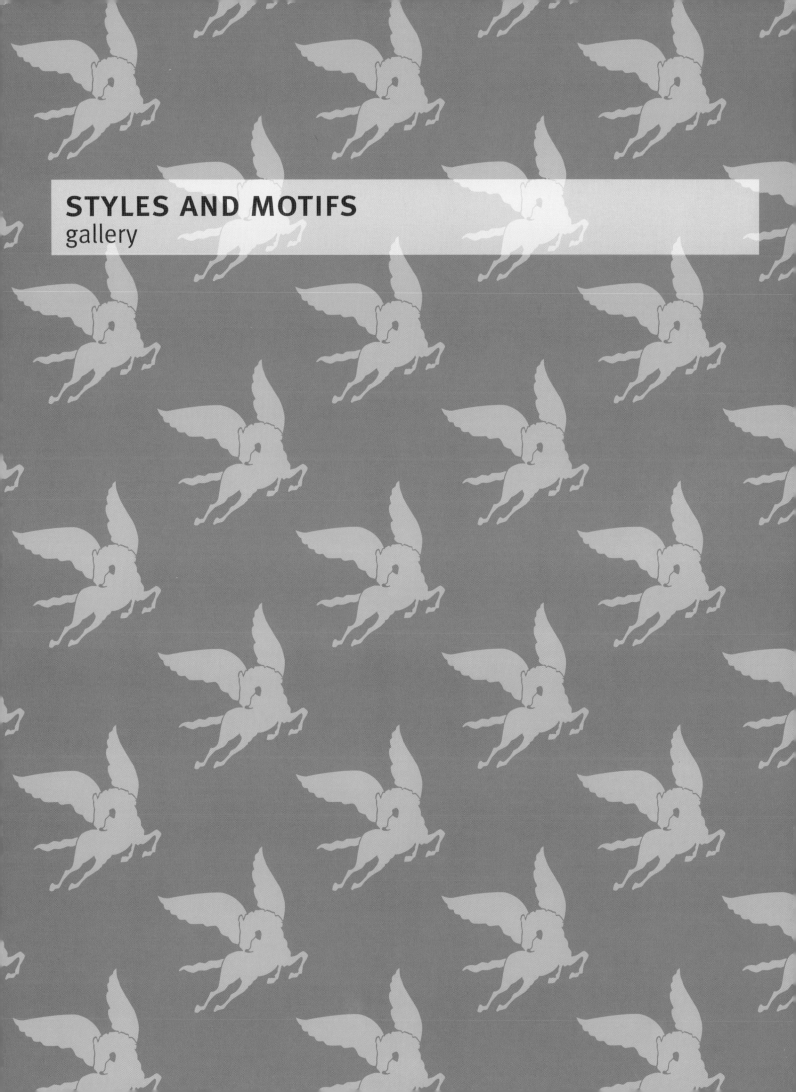

STYLES AND MOTIFS
gallery

BOTANICAL GARDEN
FLOWERS, FOLIAGE, ROMANTICISM, POP INSPIRATION

Floral and foliage motifs are a source of constant inspiration in fashion, thanks to the infinite aesthetic possibilities they present. Often, the outline and the palette of colours are what define the character of the garment and even of a complete collection. Here, for example, the small flowers and soft colours generate a romantic aesthetic, since the exciting forms and the psychedelic tones generate styles that go from pop up to ethnic exoticism.

Despite being intimately linked to nature, floral designs give great freedom to the designer for the creation of exquisite compositions, created from his imagination, which convert every garment into a piece of art.

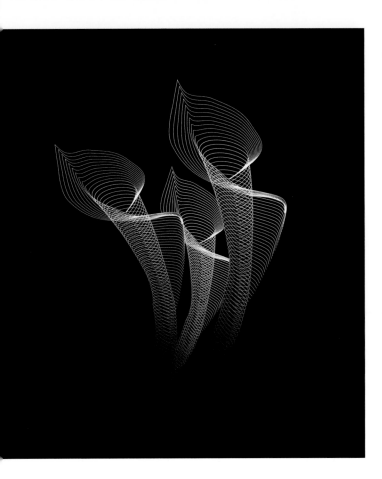

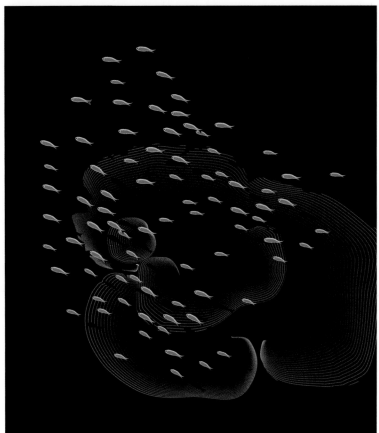

Vectorial images inspired by nature, formed by independent geometrical objects defined by different mathematical attributes of form, position, colour, etc. By Rafa Mollar.

Floral motifs are an inexhaustible source of inspiration. Here the subject is presented in a wide range of variants, from the abstract to the figurative (WGSN).

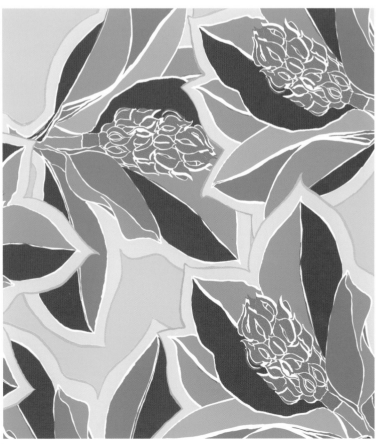

Distinct compositions in which the
creative possibilities are
appreciated by variations of size
and colour. From the firm Sisters
Gulassa.

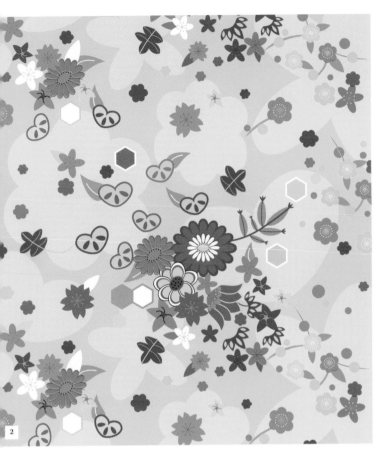

1. Positional drawing for undergarments. Spring Collection-Summer 06. By Laura Fernández.

2-3. Designs for continuous prints. Collection for bathrooms, Spring-Summer 06. From Oysho.

4-5. Positional drawings that are part of a lingerie collection. Collection Spring-Summer 06. By Laura Fernández for the firm Oysho.

GEOMETRY
LINES AND CIRCLES

Fashion designers often use geometrical forms when designing patterns for garments. Rectangles, rhombuses, trapezoids, triangles and circles acquire volume in the space and ensure that the garments gain life around the human figure. Lines in a print can generate interesting effects, to the point that they can redefine the cut of the garments, promoting aspects of the pattern making.

Thanks to their colourful and distinct design possibilities, the use of geometry in prints was taken up by the Italian designer Emilio Pucci in the 1960s. Later on, during the 1980s, following the trend that Pucci began, the Italians Krizia and Gianfranco Ferré, along with Gianni Versace, flooded the catwalks with geometrical patterns and designs and this is a trend that continues in the fashion world today.

1. The digital treatment of the figures gives rise to multiple visual effects (WGSN).

2-3. The composition based on geometric figures generates a print of ethnic style (WGSN).

4. Creation of Hanna Werning for the firm House of Dagmar. Collection Spring-Summer 2008.

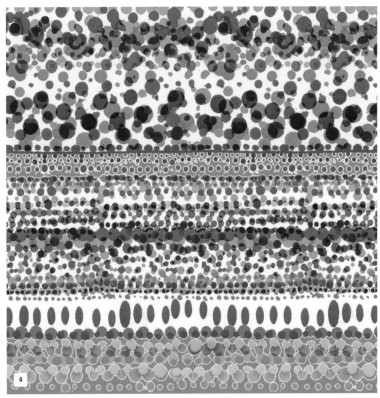

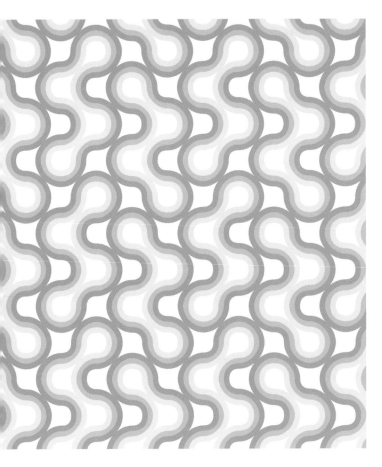

The New York designer Aimée Wilder is inspired by contemporary graphic art and by the world of design and uses this inspiration on her textile designs.

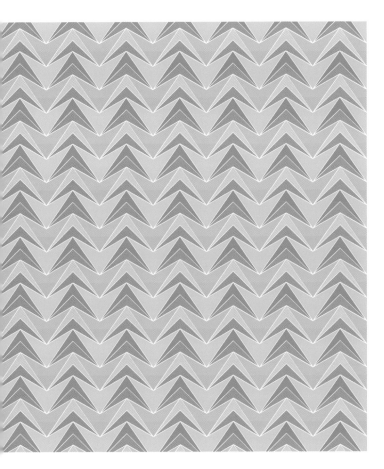

1-2-3-4. Repetition of the same figure with colour variations. By Aimée Wilder.

5-6. Geometrical designs inspired by the Japanese aesthetic tradition.

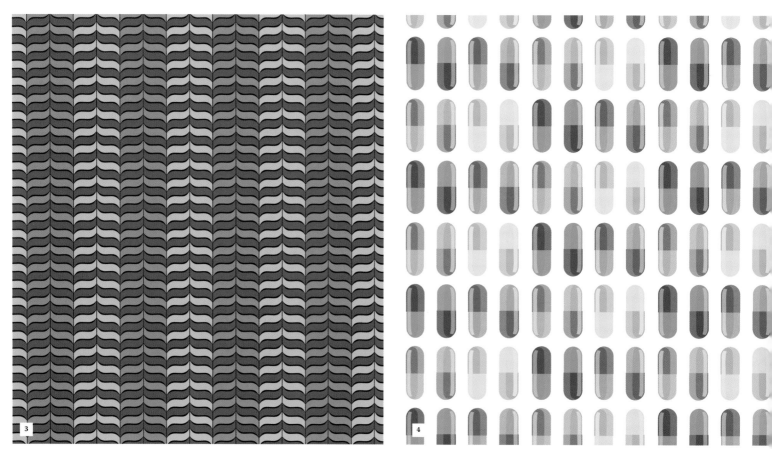

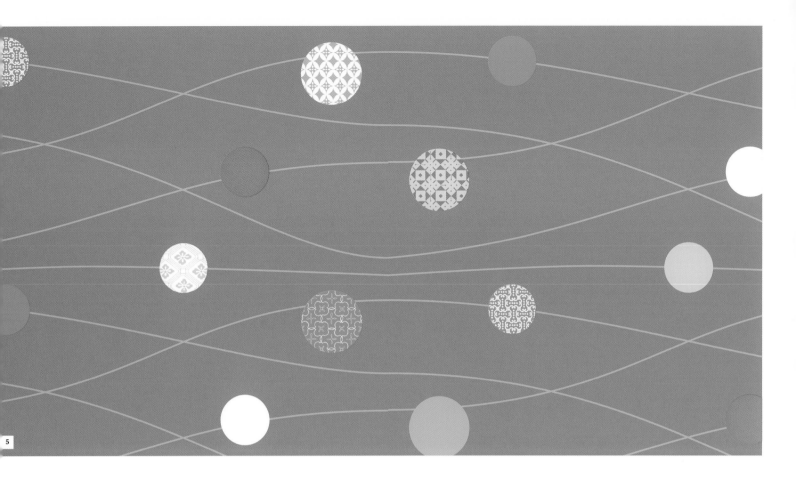

5

6

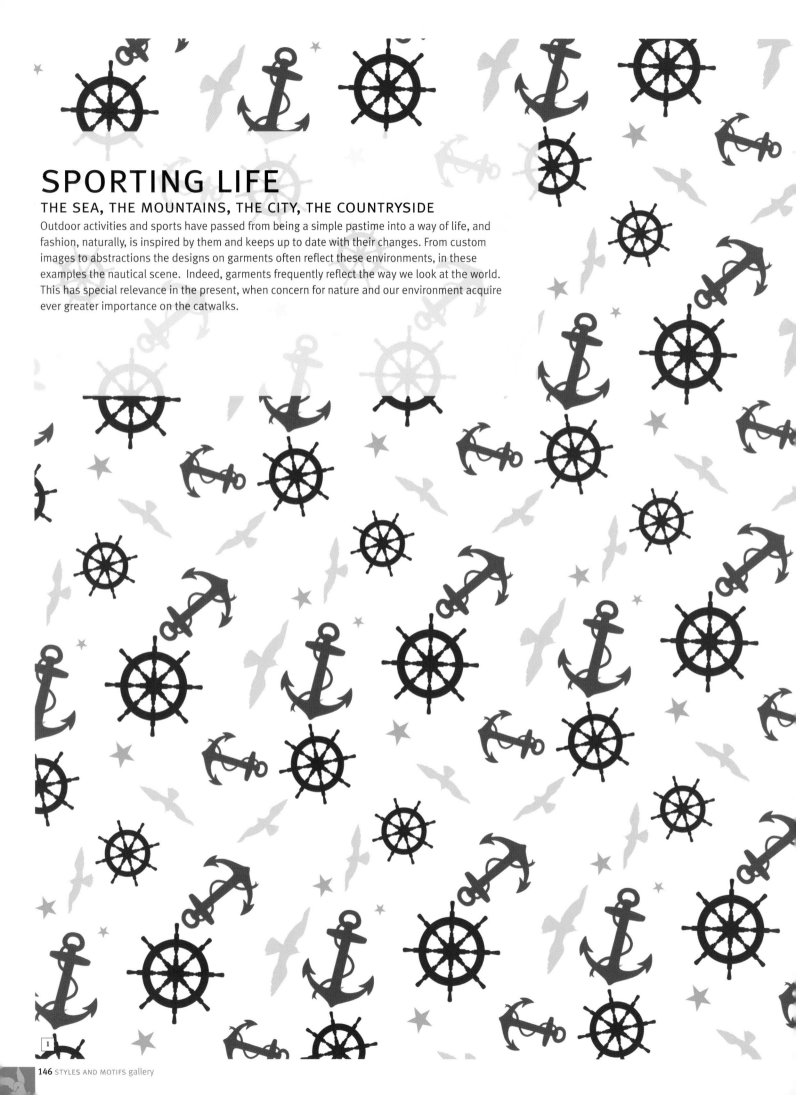

SPORTING LIFE

THE SEA, THE MOUNTAINS, THE CITY, THE COUNTRYSIDE

Outdoor activities and sports have passed from being a simple pastime into a way of life, and fashion, naturally, is inspired by them and keeps up to date with their changes. From custom images to abstractions the designs on garments often reflect these environments, in these examples the nautical scene. Indeed, garments frequently reflect the way we look at the world. This has special relevance in the present, when concern for nature and our environment acquire ever greater importance on the catwalks.

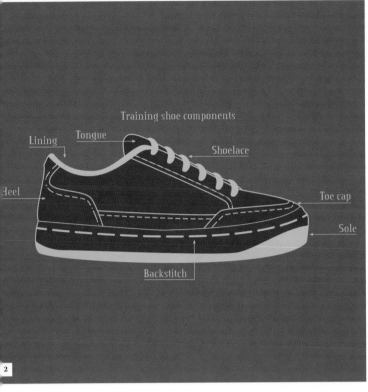

1. Nautical inspirations used for design. By Aimée Wilder.

2-3-4-5. Original drawing and applications on different garments. From the firm Giulio.

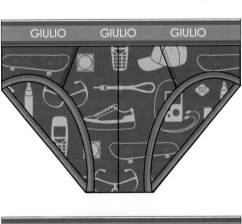

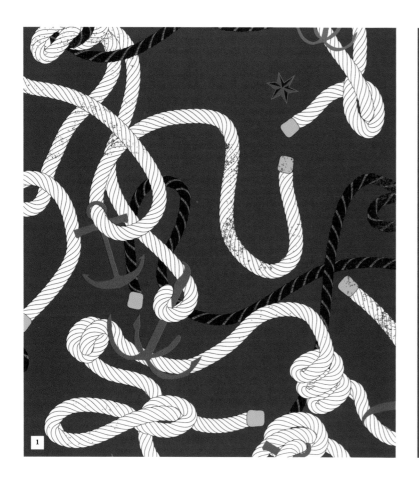

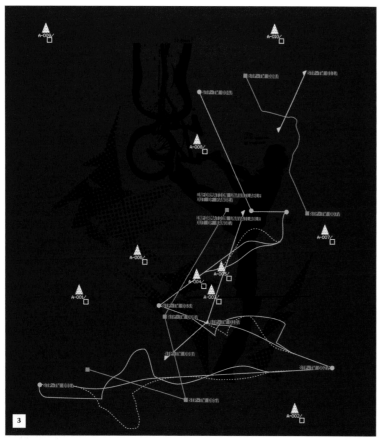

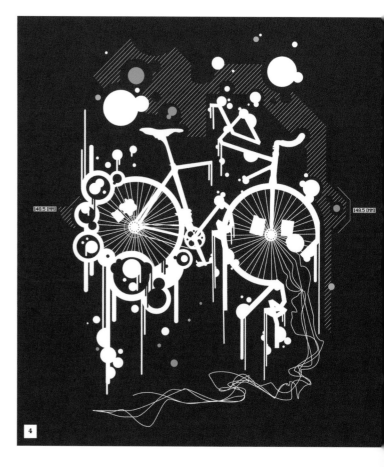

5

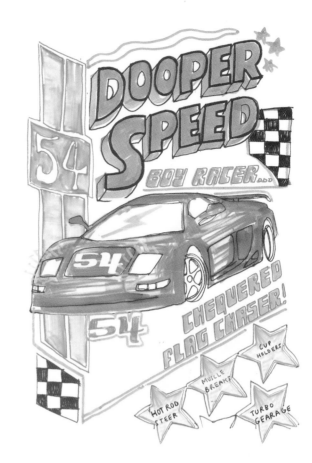

6

1-2-3-4-5. Sporting icons used for textile patterns (WGSN).

6-7-8. Illustrations for screenprinting on T-shirts (WGSN).

7

8

KULTE

THE STANDARD OF EXCELLENCE
IN ALL COLOR OF THE REAL LIFE

2

3

1. Design that combines drawings and lettering. From the firm Kulte.

2-3-4-5-6. Colours and retro typography for these illustrations of motorcycles and cars which were used on T-shirts for children.

4

5

6

FAIRY TALES
THE STORIES OF FAIRIES AND THE FABLES

Fairy stories and fables spring from worlds created by the imagination and tradition. Fairies, elves, trolls, giants and even witches and demons constitute part of the regular list of these narratives, which frequently have their origin in folklore and are represented in designs within the aesthetic influences of every period.

Although they are most often found on baby and children's clothing, the imaginative motifs, full of colour, inspired by these fabulous stories appear on prints of very diverse styles.

Drawings for T-shirts inspired by
the fables (WGSN).

1

2

1. Positional print for a girl's T-shirt that displays record covers from the 1970s.

2. Design for children's wear reflecting a 50 year old retro aesthetic.

3

4

Lost Doggie

If you find him please look after him. Thank you

5

6

3-4-5-6. Illustrations for children's clothing that are based on cartoons.

7-8. Designs inspired by candy wrappings and childhood publicity from the 1950s. By Laura Fernández.

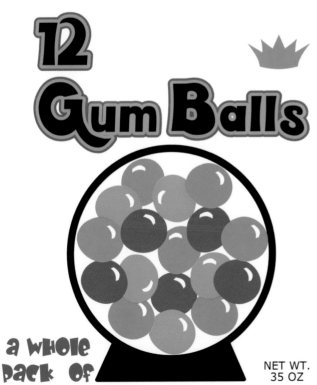

12 Gum Balls

a whole pack of

NET WT. 35 OZ

juicy flavors!

7

Star Candy

Magic Pouring Candy!!!

8

1

2

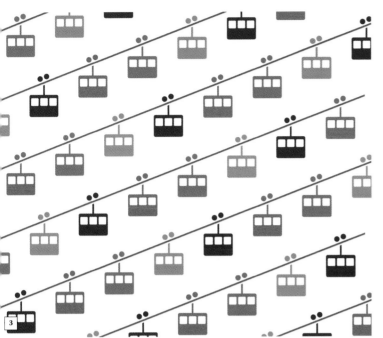

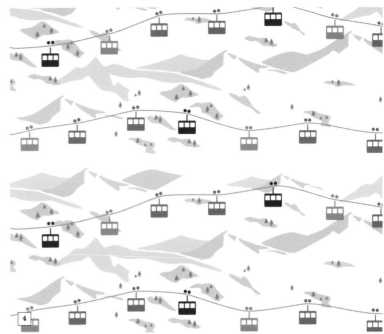

1-2. Simple line and naif motifs in design. From the firm La Casita de Wendy.

3-4-5-6-7. Continuous prints for textiles for children's clothing. By Aimée Wilder.

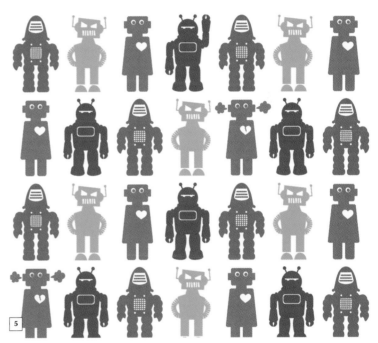

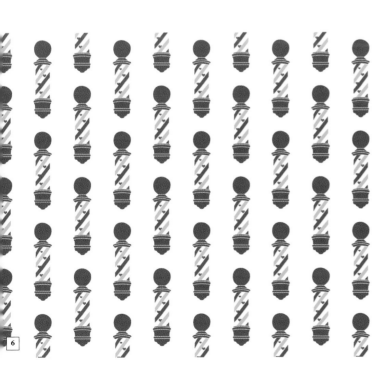

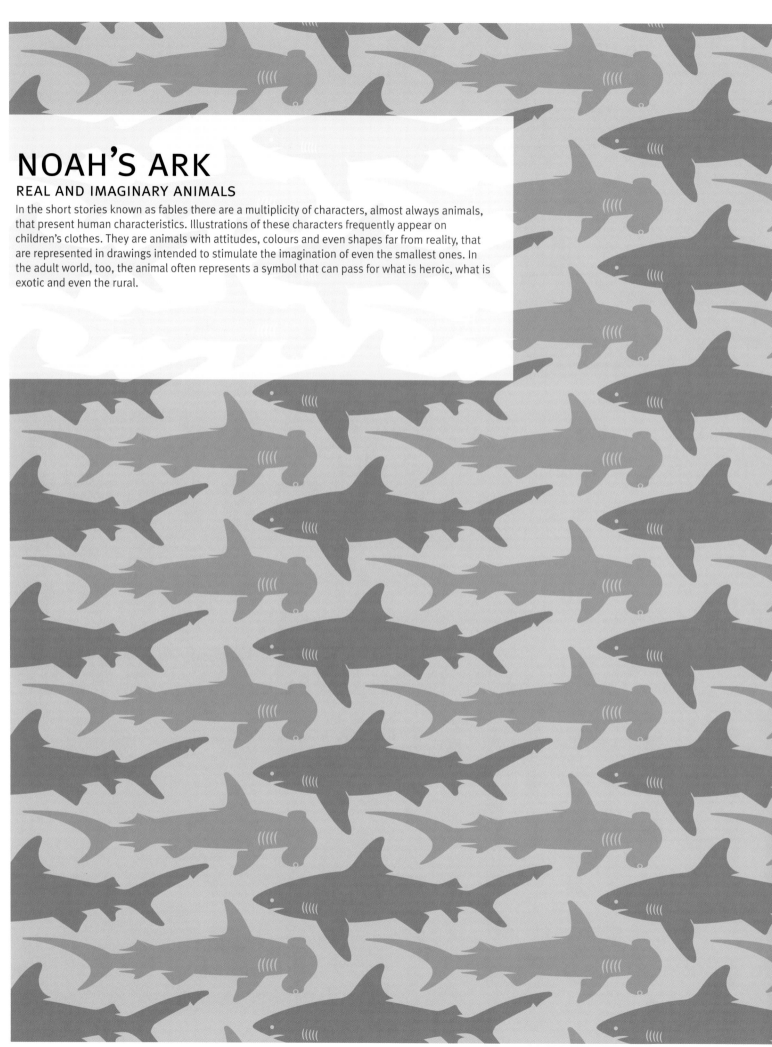

NOAH'S ARK
REAL AND IMAGINARY ANIMALS

In the short stories known as fables there are a multiplicity of characters, almost always animals, that present human characteristics. Illustrations of these characters frequently appear on children's clothes. They are animals with attitudes, colours and even shapes far from reality, that are represented in drawings intended to stimulate the imagination of even the smallest ones. In the adult world, too, the animal often represents a symbol that can pass for what is heroic, what is exotic and even the rural.

Animal figures used for continuous
prints. By Aimée Wilder.

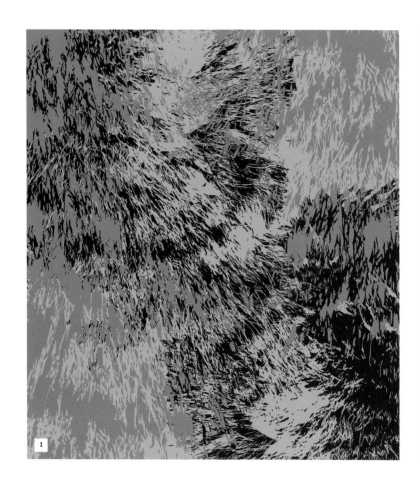

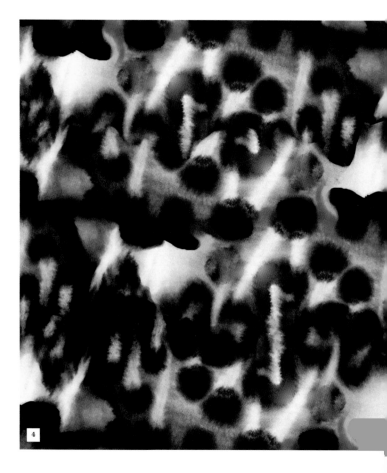

1-2-3-4. Skins of animals and feathers reproduced in an almost photographic way (WGSN).

5-6-7-8. Continuous prints from the silhouettes of animals (WGSN).

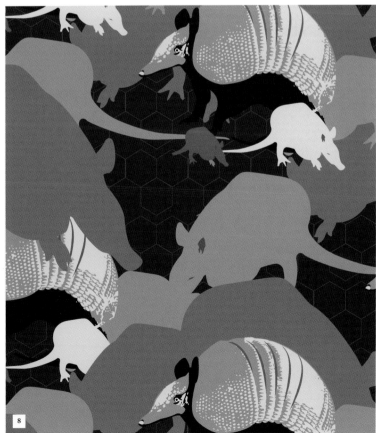

1

2

3

4

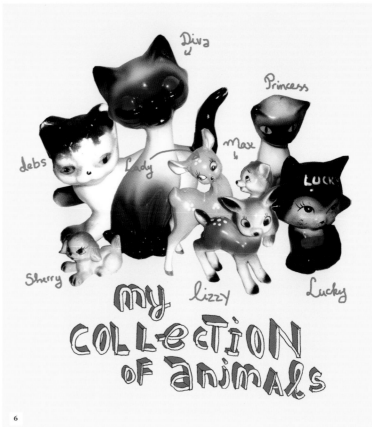

1-2-3-4-5. Positional designs of animal themes aimed at a juvenile public (WGSN).

6-7-8. Positional prints for children's clothes (WGSN).

1

2

3

1-2. T-shirts printed for the collection Perros from the firm Divinas Palabras. Collection Spring-Summer 2005.

3-4-5. Designs of the series *Loros, bats e insectos* (Parrots, bats and insects). By Laura Fernández for the firm Giulio. Collection Fall-Winter 08/09.

EXOTIC TRIPS
AFRICA, ASIA, SOUTH AMERICA

Exoticism is a taste for what is foreign. It is the search for what is different, for the unusual and for images that transport you to different worlds fed by imagination and a sense of adventure. Fed on images of distant lands and remote times, this subject transports the spirit to imaginary scenarios that appeal to the instinct for exploration and the taste for what is distinct and unusual.

In this context prints of ethnic inspiration are frequently based on the rich iconography of Africa, Asia and South America. Under this theme, year after year, the catwalks present landscapes, scenes of daily life and abstract designs that refer to forms and colours that are part of these cultures. And after passing through the eye of the contemporary designer, they are revitalised in prints full of intensity.

1

1. Design of Hawaiian inspiration. By Aimée Wilder.

2-3-4-5. Drawings of tropical flowers. By Laura Fernández for the firms Xbaby and Massimo Dutti.

2-3. Prints inspired by Arabic calligraphy. By Sisters Gulassa.

1-4-5. Forms and colours that reflect Asian cultures. Of WGSN.

1

2

1. Vectorial design for embroidery for the back and front part of a sweatshirt with hood. Collection *Cutter Lads.* By Inocuo The Sign for the firm Artful Dodger.

2. Composition inspired by the London of 1800. Collection *Cutter Lads.* From the firm Artful Dodger.

3. Exotic figures in positional drawing. Collection *Trip.* From the firm Artful Dodger.

4. Composition of hand drawings. From the firm Artful Dodger.

3

4

Drawings for a collection inspired by the hallucinations of 19th century travellers affected by unknown illnesses. From the firm Artful Dodger.

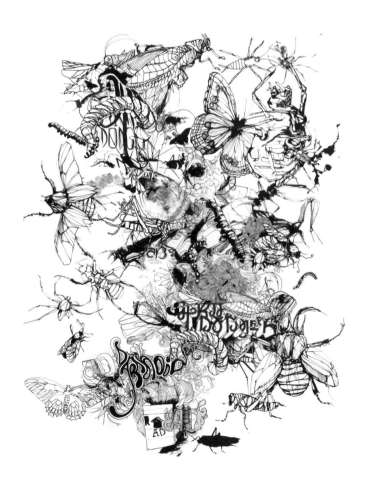

LETTERS AND NUMBERS

IDEAS AND MESSAGES

Typography plays a basic role as a source of inspiration. This vehicle of expression reached its high point with the conceptual art that reappeared with force at the end of the 1980s and that was in some cases manifested in the phrases transmitted by electronic means.

Typography as a source of inspiration, plays a basic role.Through the type size and the way the characters are used, it reinforces the message the designer wants to transmit. Calligraphic ornaments, whose origins go back to very early cultures, play a key role in this inspiration.

1

1. Illustration *New World. Hombre versus máquina* (*New World. Man versus Machine*) collection. From the firm Artful Dodger.

2. Illustration for T-shirt.

3. Inscription *Blood Sweat and Silk* for sweatshirt.

4. Logo for T-shirt.

5. Logos for back part of sweatshirt. Collection *1835.* From the firm Industrial Revolution.

1-2-3-4-5-6. The meaning of the words is reflected in the typefaces that are created for every design (WGSN).

7-8-9-10. Illustrations of screenprinted T-shirts (WGSN).

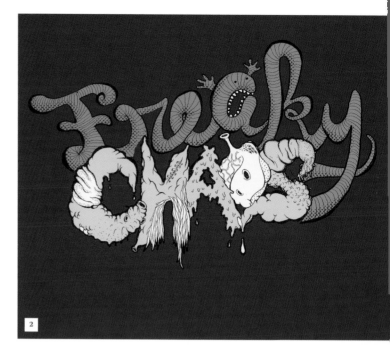

7

8

9

10

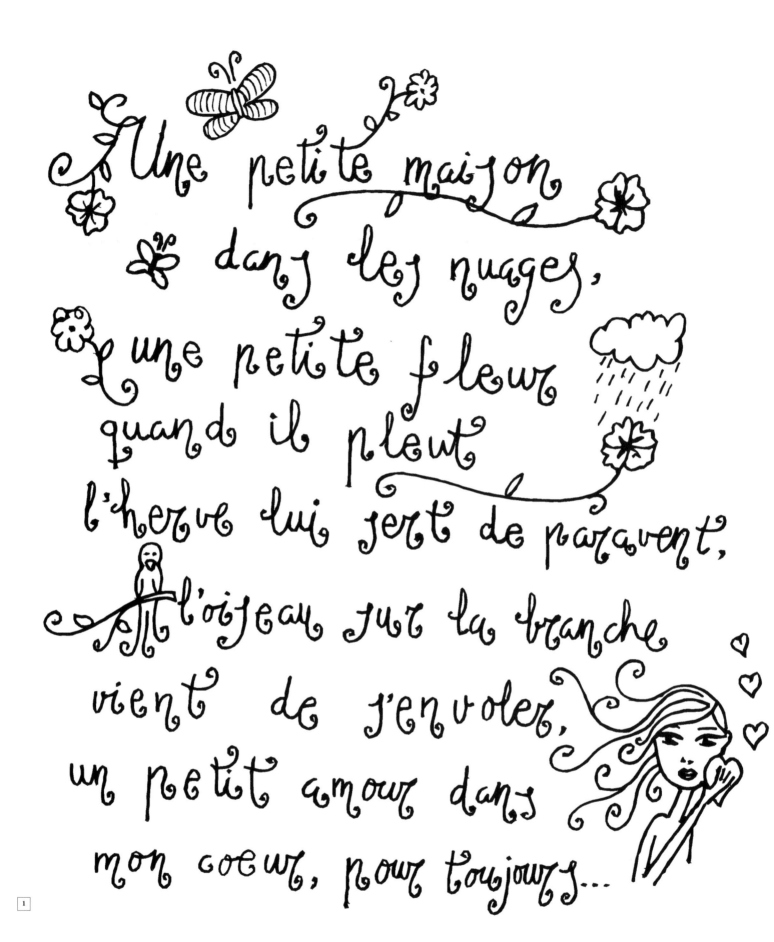

Une petite maison dans les nuages, une petite fleur quand il pleut l'herve lui sert de paravent, l'oiseau sur la branche vient de s'envoler, un petit amour dans mon coeur, pour toujours...

1

1. Design that uses French as a language to highlight romanticism.

2. Design with foliage pattern that reinforces the romantic character of the message.

3. Combination of letters and flowers used to illustrate a woman's T-shirt.

4. Design *Flowers & Skulls* that combines typography with objects.

2

SI IL EST UNE
FLEUR AU PARADIS
QU'ELLE SE PENCHE
SUR LE TERRE

fleur du paradis

3

4

ART

FROM THE BAROQUE TO THE BAUHAUS AND THE ABSTRACT

Art and fashion have been historically linked. But although both disciplines interact and are recognised as interpreters of their time, normally it is the fashion designers that transfer the world of painting to their creations. From the influence of Japanese art in the prints of the middle of the 19th century, up to the style of the Art Nouveau at the beginning of the 20th century, through the rationalism of the Bauhaus, the ironies of Pop Art and the simpleness of Minimalism, clothes can be recognised as a mobile canvas. The most sublime example of this is the iconic dress in the Autumn 1965 collection of Yves Saint Laurent that reproduced the geometrical compositions of Piet Mondrian. Also intimately linked to art, architecture has been connected more than ever to fashion in the last few years, thanks to the profound changes in the materials and construction techniques available.

1

1. Forms and colours that refer to the Pop Art movement. From the firm Sisters Gulassa.

2. Image of Bob Dylan for positional print that takes on the same aesthetics as Pop Art (WSGN).

3-4. Portraits that recur in various pictorial techniques of 20th century art (WSGN).

1

1-2-3. Illustrations inspired by the optical art (Op Art) of the 1960s (WGSN).

4. Illustration in the Art Déco style (WGSN).

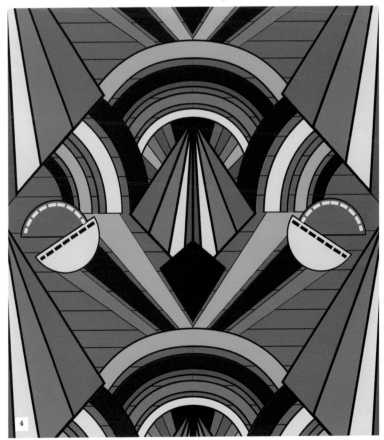

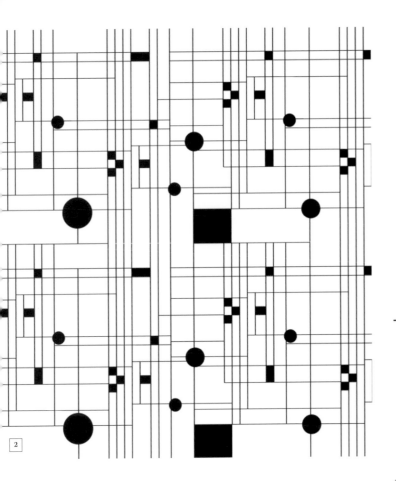

2

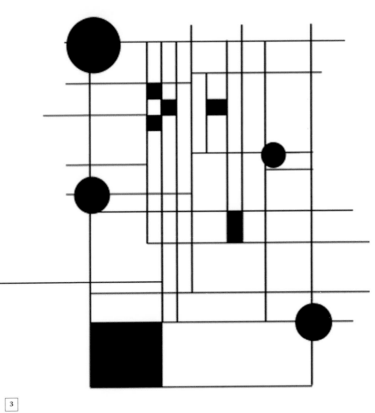

3

1. Abstract composition that reflects the aesthetics of the vanguards of the first half of the 20th century (WGSN).

2-3-4-5. Prints inspired by the symmetry and the technical rationality of Bauhaus. By Laura Fernández for the firm Giulio. Collection Winter 2008/2009.

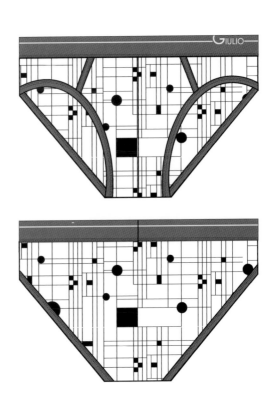

4

5

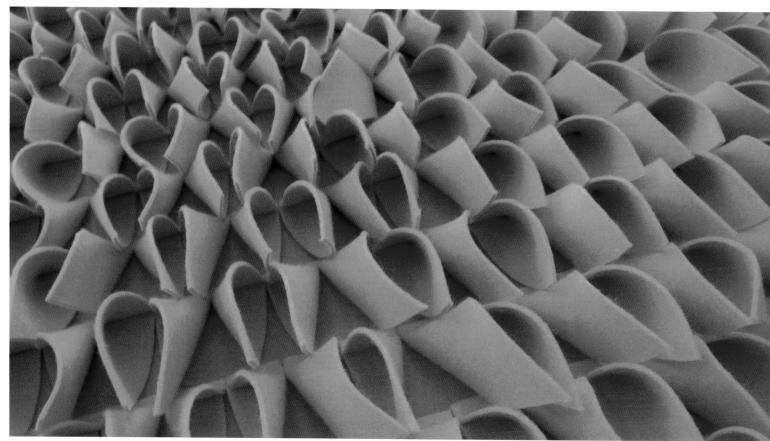

The textile designer Anne Kyyrö Quinn works with forms, volumes and textures, with an almost architectural construction.

This method reflects a new trend in embroidery, since here a drawing is not used, but instead the design is created by the manipulation of the fabric. By Anne Kyyrö Quinn.

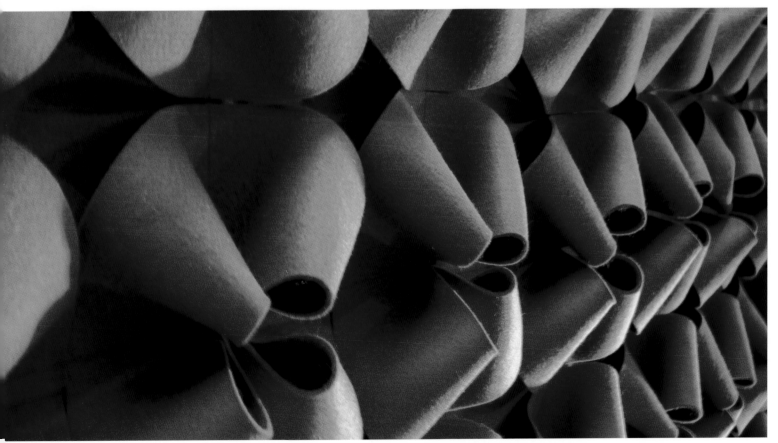

NEW ROMANTIC
DESIGNS FROM THE IMAGINATION

The origin of ornamental motifs is rooted in the symbols of various cultures from down the centuries. Rococo, Baroque, Classicism, Islamic Art, Gothic and Romanesque are only some examples of the styles which gave light to forms inspired by nature and by sublimating ancestral cultural symbols until eventually generating images of extreme beauty. In many cases they even have their origin in the spiritual plane (such as the ying and the yang in Asian culture or the sinuous forms in the Celtic culture).

1

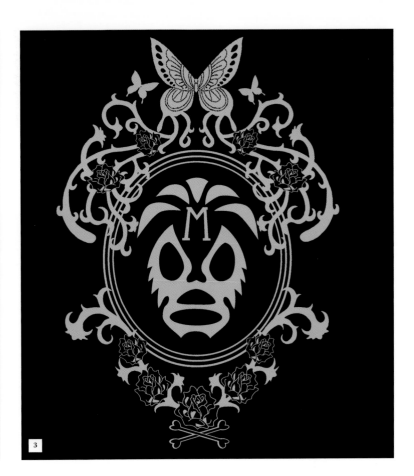

1. Positional digital design for the neckline of a woman's dress. By Laura Fernández.

2-3. Prints that reflect the iconography of death in Mexico. From the firm Mátala Mama.

4-5. Prototypes of positional prints for T-shirts. By Laura Fernández for Springfield. Fall-Winter Collection 2005/2006.

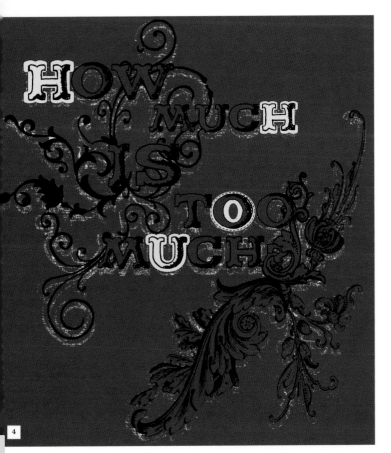

1. Original print with the slogan *Rock & Circus*. Collection Spring-Summer 2006. From the firm Mátala Mamá.

2. Inspiration for the *Art Nouveau* women's Autumn-Winter collection 05/06. From the firm Springfield.

3-4. Prototypes of positional patterns to T-shirts. Collection Autumn-Winter 05/06. From the firm Springfield.

5. Composition of musical and floral elements where the stamens are converted into microphones and musical notes into flowers. By Basso & Brooke.

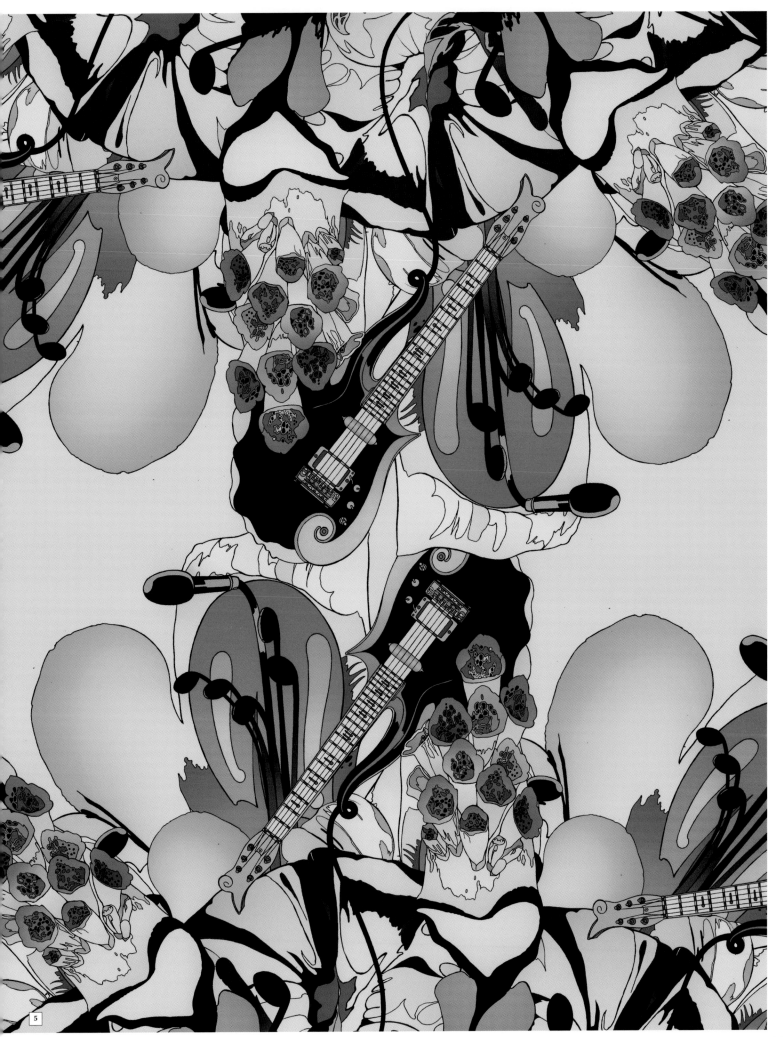

DIRECTORY

AILANTO
Diputación, 248, 3º
08007 Barcelona, España
T. + 34 93 487 06 96
ailanto@ailanto.com
www.ailanto.com

AIMEÉ WILDER
Brooklyn, NY 11211
Nueva York, Estados Unidos
info@aimeewilder.com
www.aimeewilder.com

ANNE KYYRÖ QUINN
2.06 Oxo Tower Wharf
Bargehouse St, Londres SE1 9PH, Reino Unido
T. + 44 (0)20 7021 0702
info@annekyyroquinn.com
www.annekyyroquinn.com

ATELIER LZC
2, rue M. Berthelot
93100 Montreuil, Francia
T. + 33 (0)1 42 87 81 34
celine@atelierlzc.fr
www.atelierlzc.fr

BASSO & BROOKE
Via Donizetti, 48
20122 Milan, Italia
T. + 39 02 760 591
francesca.bianco@aeffe.com
www.bassoandbrooke.com

CADENA, S.A.
Río Rosas, 3-5
28003 Madrid, España
T. + 34 91 442 60 22
cadena@cadena-sa.com
www.cadena-sa.com

CHRISTIAN DIOR
Monsieur Philippe Le Moult
11 bis, rue François 1er
75008 París, Francia
www.dior.com

DIVINAS PALABRAS
Rambla del Raval, 2 bis, 1º 2ª
08001 Barcelona, España
T. + 34 93 562 02 11
info@divinaspalabras.com
www.divinaspalabras.com

GIULIO UNDERWEAR
P. Til·lers, 3-7, 08390 Montgat
Barcelona, España
T. + 34 933 892 812
info@giulio.es
www.giulio.es

HAMISH MORROW
contact@hamishmorrow.com
www.hamishmorrow.com

HANNA WERNING - SPRING STREET STUDIO AB
Drottninggatan, 88D 1tr
SE-111 36 Estocolmo, Suecia
T. + 46 (0)70 236 57 25
hello@byhanna.com
www.byhanna.com

INOCUO THE SIGN STUDIO
Ciutat de Granada, 28 bis, 4 planta.
08005 Barcelona, España
T. + 34 93 45 031 067
hello@inocuothesign.com
www.inocuothesign.com

IVANA HELSINKI
Hämeentie, 157, 5ª planta
FI-00560 Helsinki, Finlandia
T. + 358-50-347 6131
pirjo@ivanahelsinki.com
www.ivanahelsinki.com

JAVIER NANCLARES
T: + 44 2086743967
j_nanclares@hotmail.com

JAVIER SIMORRA
Pol. Industrial Can Casablancas
Vallès, 3, Sant Quirze del Vallès
08192 Barcelona, España
T. + 34 93 721 7978
simorra@simorra.com
www.javiersimorra.com

JOSEP FONT
Ciutat de Granada, 96-98 bajos
08018 Barcelona, España
T. + 34 93 300 31 11
Gabriela@josepfont.com
www.josepfont.com

LA CASITA DE WENDY
C/ Nuria, 32, 2º B
28034 Madrid, España
T. + 34 91 702 57 85
info@lacasitadewendy.com
www.lacasitadewendy.com

LAURA FERNÁNDEZ
olivia.superstar@gmail.com
http://ladyf-f.blogspot.com
ligia unanue estudio de diseño
C/Rosalía de Castro, 59, bajos
08025 Barcelona, España
T.+ 34 93 535 05 00
nurligia@yahoo.es

LOUIS FERAUD
2, rue de Bassano
75116 París, Francia
T.+33 (0)1 49 52 44 00
contact@feraud.com
www.feraud.com

MANUEL ALBARRÁN
artmanuelalbarran@gmail.com
www.manuelalbarran.com

MARCUS JAMES
6, Compton Terrace
Londres N1 2UN, Reino Unido
T: + 07779 099 047
marcus@marcusjames.co.uk
www.marcusjames.co.uk

MARÍA JOSÉ LLEONAR
T: + 34 679 389 792
pepalleonar50@gmail.com

MIRIAM OCÁRIZ
Ribera de Axpe, 11B-L005
Erandio-Vizcaya, España
T. + 34 94 475 14 57
info@miriamocariz.com
www.miriamocariz.com

PREMIÈRE VISION PARIS
www.premierevision.fr

RAFA MOLLAR
C/ Arretes, 24-30, local 13
08001 Barcelona, España
contacto@rafamollar.com
www.rafamollar.com

SISTERS GULASSA
Backenbrunnlg. 9
1180 Viena, Austria
T. + 431 470 2490
cyrille@sistersgulassa.com
www.sistersgulassa.com

SHARON WAUCHOB
9, rue de Beauce
75003 París, Francia
T. + 33 1 42776734
contact@sharonwauchob.com
www.sharonwauchob.com

STAR – STAMPA TESSUTI ARTISTICI S.P.A.
via c. Dominioni, 2
22070 Oltrona s. Mamette 8, Como, Italia
T. + 39 031 3531 5
sales@starco.it
www.star.co.it

SYNGMAN CUCALA
Rambla Catalunya, 112
08008 Barcelona, España
http://syngmancucala.blogspot.com

VENTURES DESIGNER-SPORTS
23A, Ballygunge Place
Kolkata – 700019 India
T.+ 91 33 2440 0678/0679
sales@venturesfashion.in
www.venturesfashion.in

WGSN - WORTH GLOBAL STYLE NETWORK
C/ Aribau, 175. 3º 2ª B
08036 Barcelona, España
T. + 34 93 414 47 56
www.wgsn.com

XIMENA TOPOLANSKY DESIGN
ximenatop@bytfactory.com
www.seriallover.es

ACKNOWLEDGEMENTS

This book would not have been possible without the active collaboration and selflessness of the professionals and businesses that have supported us by sharing their work and experience.

BORDADOS EMILIO DIFUSIÓN, S.L.
Ronda Sant Elm, 37
08360 Canet de Mar. Barcelona
bordados@emiliosdifusion.com
www.emiliosdifusion.com

ESTAMPADOS LICENCIADOS S.L.
Trav. Can Maresme, 9.
Barrio Cotet, 08338 Premià de Dalt. Barcelona, España
estampados@terra.es

INDIGO PARIS
info@indigo-salon.com
www.indigo-salon.com

INSTITUT CATALÀ DE LA MODA
Gran Vía, 696. Barcelona, España
www.incatmoda.com

KARINA ZARFINO
Diseño Textil e Historia de la Indumentaria (Consulting)
T. + 34 667 867 693
karinazarfino@yahoo.es

MARCO PERI FOTOGRAFÍA
marcoperi@gmail.com

NOS & SOTO FOTÒGRAFS
C/ Lepant, 264, 6º D
08013 Barcelona, España
T.+ 34 93 2459276